What others are saying about
Touch of Joy

"One of the most important scientific discoveries of the twentieth century is that consciousness—defined as existence, awareness, and joy—is the ground of all being. *Touch of Joy* is designed to take you to the joy of unity consciousness. I strongly recommend it."

—Amit Goswami, PhD, quantum physicist and author of
The Self-Aware Universe and *The Everything Answer Book*

"I literally felt 'touched with joy' when I read this book by Jyotish and Devi Novak—a collection of the most amazing articles, which will bring immediate inspiration and satisfaction to any spiritual seeker. Examples are taken from all walks of life and all sorts of people, providing a deep authenticity. The language is simple, yet filled with deep insights that can be appreciated by anyone. I would recommend it to everyone interested in improving the quality of their lives."

—Vanamali Devi, author of *The Song of God* and *The Play of Rama*

"*Touch of Joy* brings Yogananda's remarkable legacy to everyday life. Jyotish and Devi Novak are excellent interpreters of Yogananda's teachings, having lived and imparted them for decades. No matter how much of Yogananda you've read, you will find in these pages fresh stories, shiny pearls of wisdom, and practical applications for spiritual living in today's world."

—Philip Goldberg, author of *American Veda* and *The Real Life of Yogananda*

"A treasure trove of inspiration and guidance for every possible situation—an outstanding achievement!"

—Naidhruva Rush, author of *Change Your Magnetism, Change Your Life*

"In *Touch of Joy*, Jyotish and Devi Novak beautifully express Yogananda's teachings for bringing divine grace into our daily lives. Their deep humility and discipleship, profound wisdom, and universal love for all enable them to transmit the highest teachings of yoga."

—Joseph Bharat Cornell, author of *Sharing Nature* and *Deep Nature Play*

"Gem after gem after gem. *Touch of Joy* is full of day-to-day, practical spirituality, hard-won wisdom, loving compassion, gentle humor, and soaring, joyous inspiration. Jyotish and Devi enliven my spiritual journey with grace and intelligence."

—Joseph Selbie, author of *The Yugas* and *The Physics of God*

"The ability to express deep truths simply and succinctly—and often with humor!—is a sure sign of wisdom. Jyotish and Devi Novak have been demonstrating this wisdom for years through their "Touch of Light" blog, and it is a delight to see their profound insights brought together in *Touch of Joy*. This is not a book to read through quickly and place on a shelf, but one to savor over weeks and months. Each chapter offers fresh ways and practical tips to keep one's heart and mind elevated above the assaults of noise and negativity. Together, then, these "touches" of joy can guide you to a *life* of joy!"

—Kraig Brockschmidt, author of *Solving Stress: The Power to Remain Cool and Calm Amidst Chaos*

"This book offers compact gems of wisdom that are instructive, insightful, and entertaining. I often find they address issues I'm currently working on, showing me their universal nature and helping me to live the spiritual path as a great adventure. I thank you with all my heart!"

—Lila Devi, founder of Spirit-in-Nature Essences and author of *From Bagels to Curry*

"*Touch of Joy* is delightful! I recommend you keep it close to you at all times. A dip into any one of its short articles of spiritual encouragement is like walking into a refreshingly clear and cool river on a hot day. One of my favorites pieces is 'How to Avoid Doing Your Duty,' which explains how you can do what you need to in your life, while keeping it rewarding, inspiring, and fun."

—Savitri Simpson, teacher, and author of *The Meaning of Dreaming*, *Chakras for Starters*, and other spiritually uplifting books

"I am looking forward to reading again the many thoughtful and instructive stories from two spiritual leaders so intimately attuned to Paramhansa Yogananda and Yogananda's classic *Autobiography of a Yogi*. This book is full of rare insights for everyone interested in yoga, meditation, and joy."

—Nischala Cryer, co-founder of Ananda University and author of *The Four Stages of Yoga: How to Lead a Fulfilling Life*

TOUCH of JOY

TOUCH
of JOY

A Yogi's Guide to
Lasting Happiness

JYOTISH AND DEVI NOVAK

crystal clarity **publishers**
Nevada City, California

Crystal Clarity Publishers, Nevada City, CA 95959

Copyright © 2018 by Hansa Trust
All rights reserved. Published 2018.

Printed in the United States of America

1 3 5 7 9 10 8 6 4 2

ISBN-13: 978-1-56589-325-2
ePub ISBN-13: 978-1-56589-580-5

Cover designed with love by Amala Cathleen Elliott
Interior designed by David Jensen

Library of Congress Cataloging-in-Publication Data Available

crystal clarity **publishers**
www.crystalclarity.com
clarity@crystalclarity.com
800.424.1055

CONTENTS

Introduction 10

Seven Revolutionary Teachings of Paramhansa Yogananda. 12

How Is World Peace Possible? 14

Anything Will Talk with You. 16

How to Draw God's Help in Your Life 18

Understanding Is Overrated 20

Good Judgment / Bad Judgment. 22

How to Be Friends with God 24

The Common Denominator. 26

God Is the Doer 28

Being God's Advisor 30

In Divine Friendship. 32

Why I Meditate. 34

The Benefits of Fasting 36

Where His Shadow Falls 38

Say "Yes" to Life 40

Two Bowls of Lemons. 42

The Happiness Cycle. 44

How to Be a Channel for God's Light. 46

Why Devotees Suffer. 48

Doing the Work 50

The Power of Divine Love 52

Who Is It That Dies? 54

Nine Ways to Improve Concentration 56

The Transforming Power of God's Light Within 58

Preparing for Life's Storms 60

Imitating What We Hear 62

Joy Is the Solution, Not the Reward .64

Why Is Life Such a Struggle? 66

Gratitude Brings Happiness 68

Does God Listen to Our Prayers? 70

Positive Thinking 72

God's Protecting Presence 74

Why We Need Nature 76

Is It Possible to Fail Spiritually? 78

Two Questions 80

The Yogic Lifestyle 82

Spiritual Birth 84

When God Speaks 86

The One Percent Solution 88

The Broken Connection 90

Finding *Autobiography of a Yogi* 92

Five Days in the Timeless Zone 94

Magnetizing Your Life 96

How to Defend a Principle 98

The Most Memorable Talk 100

The Dangers of Narrow Mountain Roads 102

Simple Living 104

Why Our Plans Go Awry 106

Mother, Reveal Thyself 108

Your Gifts to the World 110

Giving the Real Gift 112

The Christmas Mystery 114

The Full Moon 116

The Spark of a Spiritual Revolution 118

World Peace 120

Why Positive Thinking Changes Our Life 122

Stories as Teachers 124

Just a Play of Light and Shadows 126

The Formula for Success 128

When God Calls 130

The Monkeys of Brindaban 132

How Will Our Story End? 134

Flowers 136

The Invisible Cord 138

Full Blast 140

How to Feel That God Is the Doer 142

Self-Definition 144

Can We Change Our Future? 146

Five Essential Steps to Happiness 148

If You Want His Answer 150

Technological Yogis. 152

Weeding and Pruning 154

Swami Kriyananda, a Model for Your Life. 156

Rust Never Sleeps 158

Controlling Our Reactions 160

Moving Beyond the Ego 162

Achieving Balance in an Unbalanced World 164

From Concentration to Absorption to 166

Mountains, Outer and Inner. 168

The Treasure Box. 170

Lesson Learned, Lesson Reviewed 172

Breaking Free of Our Karma. 174

Share Your Light 176

Courage 178

The Third Wave. 180

Going Beyond the Restless Mind. 182

The Reign of King Dwaparian. 184

What Awaits Us. 186

The Golden Rule. 188

The Final Step in Discipleship. 190

A Touch of Light and Joy 192

A Dream of the Future 194

The Game 196

My Personal Journey with *Autobiography of a Yogi* 198

How *Autobiography of a Yogi* Changed My Life 201

The Banana Tree 203

How to Avoid Doing Your Duty 205

Building Spiritual Power Against Troubled Times 207

A Miracle of Protection 210

Are You a Spiritual Success? 212

Two Great Masters 214

Crossing a Threshold Opened Long Ago 216

Christmas Images and Their Spiritual Meaning 218

The Second Coming of Christ 220

How to Be a Divine Sculptor 222

About the Authors *225*

About Ananda *228*

Additional Titles from Crystal Clarity *230*

INTRODUCTION

"**W**HAT A LAUGH YOU have!" Bhaduri Mahasaya, a revered Indian saint, spoke these words to a young Paramhansa Yogananda, author of *Autobiography of a Yogi*. Having an impish, utterly delightful sense of humor, Yogananda would sometimes laugh so hard at an amusing incident that tears would flow down his cheeks.

Swami Kriyananda, his direct disciple and our lifelong teacher, told us many stories, including amusing ones, from the years he spent with the Master. Often while Yogananda was telling a joke, he would be so overcome with mirth that those present couldn't entirely understand what he was saying. Nevertheless, his waves of joy were so powerful that everyone would soon get swept away by them and begin roaring with laughter themselves.

The great master's nature was not a frivolous one, however. Swami Kriyananda said that even in the midst of hearty amusement, when he looked into Yogananda's eyes they were "so deeply calm, it seemed to me that I was gazing into infinity."

"Ever-existing, ever-conscious, ever-new bliss," or *Satchidananda*: this is how the great sages of India have described God. (It was Yogananda who added "ever-new" to the translation.) Joy is an aspect of God, and is at the heart of our own soul nature. It is not to be found in outer fulfillments or gratifications, but exists without any cause.

Swami Kriyananda once said, "Joy is the *solution*, not the *reward*." To learn to live with joy under all circumstances, and not to wait only until conditions are to our liking, is the secret of a happy life.

This book, *Touch of Joy*, is a compilation of our weekly blogs, "A Touch of Light," covering the years 2015–2016. Drawing from the teachings of Paramhansa Yogananda, we share practical tools, instructive stories, and right attitudes to help you learn to tap into the wellsprings of joy within you. (If you aren't already subscribing to our blog and are interested, you can sign up on ananda.org.)

Here are some helpful hints on how to draw the most from each individual "touch of joy" selection:

Read each one thoughtfully and slowly. Think about the core concepts until you find one that speaks to you personally. Then meditate on that thought until it percolates deep into your consciousness. Decide how you can apply it practically in your daily life. Finally, LIVE IT AND SHARE IT!

In one of Swami Kriyananda's delightful songs, we find this good advice: "The secret of laughter lies in the laughing." We hope that *Touch of Joy* will help you to find your center of joy within. Once you've learned to laugh from your heart, your joy will touch the heart of everyone you meet.

Nayaswamis Jyotish and Devi
Ananda Village
July 2, 2017

SEVEN REVOLUTIONARY TEACHINGS OF PARAMHANSA YOGANANDA

January 1, 2015

PARAMHANSA YOGANANDA'S MISSION was to help usher the whole world, with greater understanding and spiritual insight, into Dwapara Yuga, the new Age of Energy in which we live. "Someday," Swami Kriyananda wrote, "I believe he will be seen as the *avatar* of Dwapara Yuga."

It was a world-changing mission, and therefore his teachings needed to be revolutionary. In some cases what he taught was well known in India but created a revolution in the West. Others of his teachings were completely new to this age. Let's look at some of both.

1. Only God exists. God is both beyond and within all manifestation. He dreams this world into existence, and every atom and star is created from His consciousness. The goal of life is to awaken from the dream and realize our unity with Him. *Why revolutionary? This ancient Vedic teaching is new to the West, which views creation as wholly separate from the Creator.*

2. Daily meditation, stilling the mind, is the way to see behind the dream. Meditation consists of withdrawing outwardly directed prana (subtle energy or life-force) and focusing it at the spiritual eye, concentrating on God or on one of His qualities: light, sound, joy, peace, calmness, love, wisdom, or power. *Why revolutionary? When Yogananda came to America in 1920 almost no one meditated. Now millions do so daily.*

3. Prana keeps us alive, keeps us healthy, makes us magnetic, and allows us to succeed. All aspects of life are improved when we learn to control it, for to control energy is to gain control also over all things material. Yogananda taught the techniques of Kriya Yoga and the Energization Exercises to help us gain this control. He often said that the true altar is not in any church, but in our central nervous system.

Why revolutionary? The importance of life-force is only now entering the fringes of science and the healing arts.

4. Karma and reincarnation. Every thought, feeling, and action creates a wave of energy that is destined to return to us: As we give, so shall we receive. The results of our own past actions create the circumstances and events of life. The way to free ourselves from this karmic cycle is to accept life, control our reactive processes, be even-minded and cheerful, and dissolve the ego. *Why revolutionary? Appreciation of the importance of karma is beginning to sweep the world and change behavior.*

5. We don't need to leave the world. Yogananda's mission was, in part, to help us see God in every person and activity. *Why revolutionary? In the past, sincere seekers avoided worldly activity and withdrew to caves or monasteries.*

6. The desire to be happy and to avoid pain is the universal motivation behind every action. Over lifetimes our definition of what makes us happy evolves. At first happiness is sought in laziness and sensuality, then in ego-centered accumulation of possessions or power. Gradually this evolves into an altruistic desire to help others and, finally, the yearning for Self-realization, which alone brings the joy we have always sought. *Why revolutionary? People everywhere seek things, imagining that happiness lies outside themselves.*

7. Spiritual communities provide the optimal environment for the pursuit of happiness and God. *Why revolutionary? The spiritual community movement is only now starting with the Ananda communities as forerunners.*

Paramhansa Yogananda's revolutionary teachings need to be applied both culturally and personally. While these seven points only scratch the surface of what he taught, each is worth a meditation or two to see how they might apply to your life.

In the light,

Nayaswami Jyotish

HOW IS WORLD PEACE POSSIBLE?

January 8, 2015

THE MAN HAD COMMITTED MURDER many times and was now incarcerated in Tihar Prison outside of New Delhi. Yet as we watched him tell his story in the documentary *Doing Time, Doing Vipassana*, his face was peaceful and his eyes were calm.

He explained that although he'd committed many murders, he'd never felt any remorse about the lives he had taken, or even a connection between himself and his deeds. Then a new warden at Tihar introduced a voluntary program of Vipassana meditation. At first only a few prisoners participated, coming in large part to relieve the monotony.

But something started to change in these men; and others, noticing the difference, began to join in their daily meditation sessions. From a few participants, the numbers soon swelled to a few thousand, and the atmosphere of the prison began to change. The meditators began to wear fresh clothes, clean their environment, and improve the whole prison grounds. They began to serve each other, caring for those in need and helping the elderly and ill.

But more importantly, their consciousness began to change. The man in the film explained that after meditating for some months, he began to realize for the first time in his life the enormity of the sins he had committed. He prayed to God to be forgiven, and eventually was allowed to contact the family of one of his victims to beg for their forgiveness.

The victim's family came to Tihar to meet their son's murderer, and not only forgave him, but also continued to visit. After a period of time, they even legally adopted him as their son. Group practice of meditation is now being offered in prisons around the world.

I recently read about a new meditation program in some middle schools in the slums of San Francisco, California. These schools were notorious for their low attendance, low student academic performance, and so much violence that police cars were parked out-side daily.

A new principal introduced a fifteen-minute Transcendental Meditation session at the beginning and end of each day. Within a few months, student attendance was up 98%, grades had improved dramatically, and violence was almost nonexistent.

At a time when each day brings some new act of violence that claims yet more innocent lives, these stories offer great hope for the future. They provide an answer to the question: How is it possible to achieve world peace?

As in the case of the meditating prisoners and students, human consciousness must first change on an individual level before broader social changes can take place. The Dalai Lama said, "If we taught every eight-year-old to meditate, we would end war in one generation." Laws can't control violence, governments can't prevent it, nor wars stop it, because violence starts in the consciousness of the individual lost in ignorance.

Paramhansa Yogananda taught that peace must be found in the private heart through divine contact before it can be expressed in society at large. He wrote: "Toward realization of the world's highest ideal—peace through brotherhood—may yoga, the science of personal contact with the Divine, spread in time to all men in all lands."

Let us join together in this wave of social transformation, and through our practice of meditation create a spirit of global unity that can lead to lasting peace.

In divine friendship,

Nayaswami Devi

ANYTHING WILL TALK WITH YOU

January 15, 2015

GEORGE WASHINGTON CARVER, the great American botanist, said, "If you love it enough, anything will talk with you." Much more than a nice sentiment, this is a fundamental truth of the universe. But in order to communicate with nature, we need to learn new and subtle languages.

We humans communicate primarily through spoken words or written symbols, which takes a lot of initial training but, once learned, allows very rich exchanges. It also gives us the ability to pass down ideas from one generation to the next, which is vitally important. The teachings of the Vedas, the classical philosophy of the Greeks, and the words of Jesus and Krishna still live in our hearts and homes though written thousands of years ago.

We can, of course, communicate also with animals. As anyone with a pet will tell you, rich lifelong bonds are formed, filled with mutual love and joy. With animals we learn to rely more on nonverbal communication: touch, tone of voice, body language, or mental images. Some people, speaking this language better than others of us, become dog trainers, horse whisperers, and animal psychics.

In his remarkable book, *The Elephant Whisperer*, Anthony Lawrence shares how he learned to commune with wild, rogue elephants. His part was to be caring and loving. Then, he relates, they *taught him* how to communicate with them. When he died, elephants spontaneously visited his grave to say goodbye, some walking for hundreds of miles in order to pay their respects.

What about plants? A breakthrough book on this subject, *The Secret Life of Plants*, showed that surprisingly rich communications take place all the time in the vegetable kingdom. Here, the language becomes even subtler. We need to talk through kindness and listen with our hearts. Yogananda called Luther Burbank "an American saint" because of his ability to feel the common link between man and plants.

An Indian sadhu told me a remarkable story. Two weeks before I met him he had gashed his leg very badly while in the jungle. A companion, trained in herbal healing, raised his hands and began to slowly circle, explaining that he was asking the plants for help since he was unfamiliar with the plants in that area. After some time a tree "volunteered" its healing powers and he made a poultice from the leaves. Now, two weeks later, I could see only the faintest of scars from the gash.

Nor does communication end with the animals and vegetables. Yogananda wrote about J.C. Bose, a leading physicist, biologist, and botanist who showed that a common thread of awareness extends even into the mineral world. Many people communicate with gems and crystals, and the Japanese scientist, Masaru Emoto, has shown that music and thoughts can influence the very shape of water crystals.

And it doesn't stop there. A principle of modern quantum physics says that the universe at the level of its most fundamental constituents responds to consciousness! Our thoughts reach to the world of subatomic quanta and influence the universal energy field that some call "zero point energy."

When we consider all this objectively it leads us to the inevitable conclusion not only that are we connected to everything in the world, but also that we can communicate if we learn the right language. If we return to Carver's statement, we see that the universal language is love. Why? Because it is God, residing at the heart of all things, who is constantly whispering to us through them, and love is His native tongue.

In that love,

Nayaswami Jyotish

HOW TO DRAW GOD'S HELP IN YOUR LIFE

January 22, 2015

A FRIEND OF OURS in India told us a very interesting and instructive story. Indu is a lawyer, and at the time these events took place, ran a large legal firm that represented some international companies.

One of his clients ran into entanglements, including being unable to transfer funds overseas. As a result, they couldn't pay their suppliers or manufacture the goods that their customers had already paid for and needed. No matter what Indu did, he couldn't untangle the knot, and the situation went from bad to worse. After three years, the government authorities stepped in and threatened to close Indu's firm down.

Indu and his family are deeply devotional, and their lives were blessed by a great saint, Narayan Swami. Looking at the possibility of losing everything, Indu went in desperation to his guru to explain the situation and seek his help.

After listening to the problem, Narayan Swami asked him, "Do you surrender your life to me?"

Not knowing where else to turn, Indu replied, "What choice do I have?"

The Guru asked him again, but more strongly, "Do you surrender your life to me?"

Our friend repeated in desperation, "Sir, what choice do I have?"

Regarding Indu closely and with great power, Narayan Swami asked a third time, "Indu, do you surrender your life to me?"

This time he replied with a resounding, "YES!"

The Guru smiled and said, "Good. Now I can help you."

The next day at a gathering of friends, Indu met an executive secretary for a law firm based in America. She began telling him of the problems her boss was having, and Indu realized that he and the American lawyer could provide each other with the solutions that each of them needed. Within a few weeks, everything was resolved to the satisfaction of everyone concerned.

What can we learn from Indu's story? When his reply to his guru was defeatist and passive, his guru couldn't help him. But with his affirmative and energetic "YES," Indu opened the door for Narayan Swami to begin working with the subtle laws that govern this universe.

In Paramhansa Yogananda's book, *Whispers from Eternity*, he gives a wonderful explanation of the difference between beggarly prayers and prayer demands. When we passively plead for God's help, we don't generate enough focused energy to draw His response. But when, with positive faith, expectation, and inner power, we *demand* His answer, then we will receive it.

Our part in drawing God's help is to be active, not passive; affirmative, not negative; and certain, not hesitant. Yoganandaji writes in his *Whispers*, "To know how and when to pray correctly, according to the nature of your demands, is what will, and cannot fail to, bring desired results. When the demand is made rightly — not selfishly, but in a self-giving way — it will set in motion in your favor the very laws of God."

With joy,

Nayaswami Devi

UNDERSTANDING IS OVERRATED

January 29, 2015

EARLY IN MY SPIRITUAL QUEST, Swami Kriyananda was trying to help me balance a tendency to be overly rational. He patiently explained what I needed to do, and I said, "I understand, Sir." He replied, kindly but firmly, "I don't care whether you understand or not, I want you to change."

I've never forgotten that bit of advice, and it illustrates a mistake made by many. We don't have to understand something in order to change it, anymore than we need to understand electricity to be able to change a light bulb. In fact, analyzing situations is often a defense mechanism the ego uses to protect itself from needed change.

The quest for knowledge has its place. It is helpful on the material plane and can get us a diploma or a job. But, as seekers, we are trying to transcend this plane, and for us the realm of reason is too restrictive. A hot-air balloon can lift us above the hills, but it cannot take us to the stars.

People who are too rational may actually hinder their spiritual growth. They can suffer from a "Zeno" complex. Zeno was a Greek philosopher who posed this paradox: For an arrow to hit a target, it must move from the bow to the target. But, in the minutest instant of time, the arrow is frozen and unmoving. If the arrow is motionless at every instant, and time is entirely composed of instants, then motion is impossible. I've known people who spend so much time analyzing things that, if not frozen in time, at best they plod slowly and timidly through life, becoming dry and forgetting to enjoy the here and now.

What we really need is not mental understanding but wisdom, which entails the marriage of head and heart. Normally wisdom grows gradually, as the mind learns discrimination, and as the heart becomes expanded by love and softened through pain. A shorter path to wisdom can be found by concentrating at the spiritual eye in deep, silent meditation, and by attuning oneself to a truly wise guru.

At times we need to toss thinking aside and let activity become our teacher. Swami Kriyananda encouraged me to paint because, as he put it, "It will help you develop your intuition." He knew that unleashing the creative flow would lift me above the dry desert of an overactive intellect.

Just as a snake must shed its old skin, we grow by casting off old self-definitions. We already have what we seek: We have been one with God since the very first breath of creation. We don't need to learn anything in order to know Him, but only to remember and realize what we truly are. Open your heart to Him, and He will come. When we still the tumult of thought and eddies of emotion, it is then we can hear His whispers. In this eternal quest, understanding is overrated.

In divine friendship,

Nayaswami Jyotish

GOOD JUDGMENT / BAD JUDGMENT

February 5, 2015

THERE IS A HUMOROUS but instructive story in which a young man asks a wise, older gentleman for advice: "How is it that you have such good judgment?"

The sage slowly reflects, and then says, "Good judgment is born of experience."

Not entirely satisfied with this answer, the young fellow pursues his questioning: "Well, how do you get experience?"

The voice of wisdom replies dryly: "Bad judgment."

Simply put, this is the essence of the law of karma. Through ignorance, which causes us to act with bad judgment, we err and suffer. Slowly over time we acquire the experience to know, for example, that if we put our hand on a hot stove, we'll get burned. Eventually, when faced with this option, the good judgment born of experience will remind us of our past suffering, and we'll avoid it.

Paramhansa Yogananda wrote that all of life's experiences are for our education and entertainment. "But," he added a little ruefully, "how few are either educated or entertained." In this never-ending school of life, we will keep drawing lessons, moving up grade by grade, until we perfect our understanding to reflect God's wisdom.

The enlightened teachers, or satgurus, who come to help us find spiritual freedom, know what lessons we need in order to expiate our karma. Through their guidance and grace, they can prepare us for the challenges our karma has drawn. Our teachers can't, however, take the tests for us, nor shield us from them. When the lessons come, we must face them ourselves.

There is a story from the life of Lahiri Mahasaya, one of the great gurus in our spiritual lineage, in which he is walking home with one of his disciples after bathing in the Ganges. At a certain point, Lahiri stops and asks him, "Can you tear off a piece of cloth from your dhoti?"

The disciple, not understanding his guru's request, continues on. After they walk a few more steps, a brick from an overhead terrace falls and grazes one of Lahiri's toes. Unperturbed, Lahiri tears off a strip of cloth from his dhoti and, with the help of his disciple, binds his bleeding toe. His disciple asks, "If you knew that this was going to happen, Guruji, why didn't you avoid it? Then you wouldn't have suffered this injury."

The Master replied, "That is not possible. If I had avoided it, I would have had to suffer the pain at another time—with interest! I have to receive what is destined; therefore, the earlier it is completed, the better it is." In truth, Lahiri was an avatar with no karma of his own, but he was teaching the disciple and all of us the lesson of willingly facing our karmic tests.

When we err in judgment and bring suffering to ourselves, the best response is not to despair or to wallow in self-recrimination and guilt. It's far better to rejoice in the fact that through experience we're learning the life lessons we need, and are taking our next step toward inner freedom.

Wishing you joy on your journey,

Nayaswami Devi

HOW TO BE FRIENDS WITH GOD

February 12, 2015

MANY PEOPLE HAVE a very complex relationship with their Heavenly Father/Mother, just as they do with their earthly parents. In fact, many attitudes and complexes toward God are simply projections of feelings experienced when growing up. Those from harsher backgrounds can see God as disapproving and vengeful, while those raised in loving and tolerant homes tend to see a loving God. Yet even the most loving parents can be misjudged.

When our son was six years old, we took him to see the classic movie *E.T.*, about a small, frightened alien who was secretly helped by the children of a family. The scary men from the federal government and the scientists in protective suits didn't frighten our son at all. But when the little alien opened a refrigerator, dropped a carton of orange juice, and spilled it all over the floor, our son covered his eyes and said, "The mommy is going to catch him."

While we might chuckle at his reaction, there are many people who fear God because they're subconsciously afraid that the Divine Mother is going to punish them for some trifling fault, or catch them with their hand in the cookie jar of self-destructive habits and bad attitudes.

How do we develop a sincere friendship with God? Most important are the practices of meditation and devotion. Here also are three other ways that have helped me:

Stay Positive. Thoughts are universally rooted, meaning that we tune the radio of our mind to a particular wavelength. Our preset stations —habitual reactions—determine our emotional "specific gravity." If you are even-minded and cheerful, you will float on the surface of life, while those who are grumpy and judgmental will be pulled down into the depths. *But we can choose to change these mindsets.* Positive actions will generate positive thinking. Studies show that those with sunny outlooks are not only happier, but also more successful.

Try the simple practice of thinking something positive about a person you are about to mentally criticize, and see if it doesn't change your life.

Non-attachment. Most unhealthy attitudes grow from attachment. Free yourself by offering everything back to God. See each desire as a cord that binds you: Cut it, and soar into the skies of freedom. Tithing is a very powerful spiritual practice because it helps us release our anxiety and attachment to money.

Share little things with God or Guru. Don't leave your guru hanging on the wall of your meditation room. Paramhansa Yogananda said, "To those who think me near, I will be near." Bring him with you when you work, or cook, or go for a walk. Talk to him mentally and share you hopes and fears as you would with your best friend. If you see him by your side in little things, you will know he's there when the going gets rough.

God is already our friend, in fact our own Self, and that will never change no matter what we think or do. But when we befriend Him in return, our inner joy begins to bubble to the surface.

In joy,

Nayaswami Jyotish

THE COMMON DENOMINATOR

February 19, 2015

THE CHEMOTHERAPY DRUG slowly dripped into my friend's arm as we sat in the treatment room. She had been diagnosed some months earlier with an aggressive form of breast cancer, and, after surgery, was receiving a regime of outpatient chemotherapy treatments.

The room in which we sat was a large, airy space with about two dozen comfortable reclining chairs where people were receiving their intravenous treatment. The patients were from a broad cross section of society: young and old, rich and poor, men and women, alone or with family and friends. But all were there because they had hope that they could avoid the suffering of advancing cancer and find happiness once more in a disease-free life.

Paramhansa Yogananda said that everyone in this world shares one common motivation in life: to avoid suffering and find happiness. Everything we do is a higher or lower expression of this same shared goal. For some, happiness means chasing the will-o'-the-wisp of material desires or achieving recognition in the eyes of the world. For others, it's to serve those in need and lessen their suffering. And for a few, it means finding the source of true happiness: the bliss of God.

Even as we ascend the ladder of wakefulness in God, we still share with all humanity—with all life, in fact—that same twofold motivation: to avoid pain and to find happiness. Knowing this, it's much easier to see behind the multifarious expressions of human behavior and feel compassion and kinship with everyone.

As my friend and I sat together that day, she gradually drifted off to sleep, and I picked up some knitting that I'd brought along with me. As I began the rhythmic process of moving the yarn over and under the needles, one of the other patients in the room started walking towards me, pushing her IV bag and drip tube on its mobile pole.

She was an older woman, alone, and after she sat down in an empty chair next to me, she began speaking in a thick German accent.

"I haven't seen anyone knitting in a long time," she began. "You see, when I was a little girl during World War II, my family lived on a small farm in northern Germany. We were starving, because all the food was sent to the troops, and we were always cold because our clothes were threadbare and filled with holes.

"When the American paratroopers began landing behind our military lines, they would abandon their silk parachutes in the woods. My family would search for the 'chutes,' tear the silk into strips, and then knit them into warm clothing. We were so grateful to the soldiers for such gifts."

We talked on during that long afternoon. Our experiences in life had been very different, and yet as children of our one Father/Mother, God, we had so much in common and so much to share.

Towards Oneness with all,

Nayaswami Devi

GOD IS THE DOER

February 26, 2015

You never know when the universe is going to give you an important piece of the puzzle. This happened one time when Devi and I were with Swami Kriyananda in, of all places, a shopping mall in Sacramento, California. He had gotten a letter from someone who was discouraged after comparing his own accomplishments to those of Swamiji's. (Aside: Comparing ourselves to great souls is fruitless and should come with a warning label: "Do not try this at home.")

Swamiji's response was very instructive. He said, "People shouldn't be discouraged. They need to understand that I've just been at it a little longer. Everyone will find God in the end."

Many people deal not only with feelings of inadequacy, but also with the feeling that they are losing the battle against life's pressures to perform, and the accompanying stress. Growth requires a struggle—this is the lesson of the Bhagavad Gita—but we don't need to compound external pressures with internal resistance. When we accept our challenges without feeling that they are unfair, most of our resistance vanishes. That resistance is born of self-absorption. As we overcome it, life becomes happier and, finally, joyful. One of the best ways to do so is to expand our sense of self by serving others. There is a lovely passage that has been attributed to Rabindranath Tagore: "I slept and dreamt that life was joy. I awoke and saw that life was service. I acted and behold, service was joy."

There is also a deeper, more spiritual layer. Ultimately, we don't do anything. God does it all. He is the dreamer of the whole universal drama. Once we truly grasp this truth, beyond mere affirmation, all the angst and pressures of the human condition burst like a soap bubble. One night I dreamt that I was pushing a bus up a long hill. No matter how hard I struggled, I couldn't get it to move more than a foot or two. When I awoke in the morning, I saw all that work to have been only a dream. So long as we see ourselves as the doer, however, the spiritual path seems like pushing that bus.

A friend sent this quote from Anandamayee Ma: "You think that you are engaging in sadhana, but actually it is He who does everything, without Him nothing can be done. And if you imagine that you receive according to what you do, this is not correct either, for God is not a merchant; with Him there is no bargaining."

This is deeply comforting and reassuring. We don't need to accomplish anything. We just need to awaken from the dream of ego. That is both our challenge and our goal. All else is God's lila.

In joy,

Nayaswami Jyotish

BEING GOD'S ADVISOR

March 5, 2015

I READ A WONDERFUL STATEMENT recently by the British author C.S. Lewis: "Many people want to serve God, mostly in an advisory capacity."

At least some of the time, most of us think God needs our advice on rearranging things more to our liking. When everything is going well, we think He's doing a pretty good job of managing the cosmic drama, but when adversity comes, we begin to question His judgment.

Paramhansa Yogananda said that the reason God doesn't appear to most people is that they would only argue with Him! It takes spiritual maturity to surrender our life to a Higher Power and to trust that everything is happening for the best.

In 1976 Ananda Village was devastated by a forest fire, which destroyed much of the community property and burned down most of the houses. Jyotish and I lost our home and everything we owned in the blaze, which struck just eleven days after our son had been born.

Shortly afterwards, Swami Kriyananda sent us a note saying that he was sorry for our losses and for the challenges it presented at that time particularly. He added, however, "Always remember: What God gives, we take."

Swamiji offered no wishful thoughts that we might have been spared this test. He reflected to us only the courage and wisdom of a true disciple who knows that God always guides our life to the highest end.

Over time the experience of the fire proved to be a blessing for us, bringing to the fore new levels of inner strength and acceptance. In the aftermath of the blaze, however, those who felt that God was in need of some serious advice soon left.

How do we stop offering God our opinion and accept His will? Here are some thoughts:

1. Develop an attitude of openness. Don't impose your desires or expectations on life, but listen sensitively to what is trying to happen and be receptive to the flow of events. Accept, appreciate, and attune to the wisdom behind all circumstances.

2. Focus on the Dreamer behind the dream. The essence of God's consciousness is love and joy. Try to feel these eternal qualities present behind everything that happens, and know that the dream is but a passing show. Especially in the face of tests, try to feel His loving presence smiling at you.

3. Live in surrender to God and His appointed guide for us, the guru. In the vow of discipleship written by Swami Kriyananda, it says: "I have walked with the thought, 'I want this from life; these answers; that guidance; this pathway, or that,' but I have seen that, as often as I made claims on life, it eluded me. As often as I presumed on Thy will, it turned away from me."

The spiritual path, which can seem so complicated at first, ultimately reveals itself as simply living in openness and trust in God. When we are able to do this, we cease being His stern advisor and start becoming His blissful child.

In divine friendship,

Nayaswami Devi

IN DIVINE FRIENDSHIP

March 12, 2015

A COMPILATION OF OUR BLOGS has just been released in India in book form, entitled *Touch of Light: Living the Teachings of Paramhansa Yogananda*. As we travel from city to city to offer programs here, we've been "launching" the book after our discourse with a simple ceremony: a copy is brought to us tied in a bright ribbon, which we cut or untie, and then present to a dignitary. At the end of the program, books are offered for sale, and many of the attendees ask us to sign their copy. We generally inscribe it, "In divine friendship," above our signatures. This is also the closing that Swami Kriyananda would use to end his letters. Divine friendship is, in a very real sense, the core vibration of Ananda Sangha.

There are two main differences between divine and human friendship. The first is that the Divine, having no ego, has no boundaries. There is no "best friend," nor anyone excluded from the warm embrace of love—*not anyone*. When our granddaughter, Riley, was about 10 years old, her two best friends got into an argument, and each of them demanded that Riley "unfriend" the other. This she refused to do. Unwilling to choose between them, she found herself eating lunch alone each day until their little tiff lost its steam.

Human love can be divisive, but the Divine never asks us to be exclusive. In fact, it's quite the opposite, because God requires that we give love to all. As Paramhansa Yogananda wrote in his poem *Samadhi*, "The sparrow, each grain of sand, fall not without my sight." We don't need to love people's ignorant deeds, but we still need to love them—the soul.

Secondly, divine friendship is impersonal. One time Swami Kriyananda told Devi, "No one is special to me. I'm not even special to myself." At first this may seem a bit cold, but the deeper you go, the warmer it gets. Being "special" is a quality of the ego, which separates. When nothing is separate, everything becomes special: every person; every king or beggar; every flower, be it rose or weed. Because Swami Kriyananda had no boundaries to his friendship, many people, even those who saw him only on rare occasions, thought of him as their dearest friend.

"I see all of you as images of light," Paramhansa Yogananda once said to a group of his disciples. "Everything—the grass, the trees, the bushes—everything I see is made of light. You've no idea how beautiful it all is!" Let's hold this thought in our hearts. We have no idea how beautiful each one of us is to the Divine. And let's share that precious gift as well as we can. Let's see the innate beauty in everyone and everything. Then the whole world will become our friend.

In divine friendship,

Nayaswami Jyotish

WHY I MEDITATE

March 19, 2015

"I'D REALLY LIKE to practice meditation, but I just don't have the time in my busy life," is a comment people often make to us. We need to understand that just as the physical body needs food and water to survive, the soul needs the sustenance drawn from meditation to flourish. Once we begin this practice in our life, we realize that we can't survive properly without it. Then we *make* time for meditation, because our soul craves it.

For forty-six years now I've been practicing daily meditation, and I know what it has done for me. Let me share with you why I meditate:

I meditate because life can be overwhelming in its outer intensity and demands. My energy becomes depleted and dissipated unless I withdraw to the calm center of my being to refresh and recharge.

I meditate because the complexity and fractured nature of the world makes concentration almost impossible. I love to feel the power of a focused mind, and to bring this concentration to everything I do, perceive, and feel.

I meditate because the sorrows and losses I experience in life sometimes bring great pain to my heart. Friends and loved ones can offer me some solace, but I find true, lasting comfort and peace only in offering my pain into God's loving presence.

I meditate because the joys and fulfillments in life are also sometimes more beautiful than I can bear. I need to sit quietly and thank God not only for His gifts, but most especially for His constant love.

I meditate because I feel confined and limited when all I experience of myself is my ego. I love the freedom of knowing that I am but a small spark of a much greater reality.

I meditate because questions and decisions arise every day that need wisdom and subtlety to address properly. When I offer these problems to God during meditation, I often receive an answer that is the perfect solution, one my limited mind would never have perceived.

I meditate because it centers my mind on God, and allows me to pray for others with greater effectiveness.

I meditate because there is a wellspring of love in my heart that yearns to flow to and merge with the ocean of God's love.

I meditate because when my mind is calm and interiorized, I feel my Guru's presence guiding and blessing me.

I meditate because it is the only way that I can know that I am a bubble of God's joy.

With deepest joy,

Nayaswami Devi

THE BENEFITS OF FASTING

March 26, 2015

I'M FEELING BETTER TODAY. I fasted yesterday, in part to help clear out some respiratory congestion I've had since we got back from India a few days ago. For this particular purpose, I did a fast called the "Master Cleanse," in which you drink a "lemonade" consisting of lemon juice, Grade B maple syrup, and a little cayenne powder, diluted with water. Occasionally Devi and I will do Paramhansa Yogananda's marvelous Nine-Day Cleansing and Vitalizing Diet, which consists of lots of citrus, raw vegetables, a daily steamed vegetable, and a special "vitality beverage."

I noticed during our trips to India that fasting is much more common there. We often encountered people who declined food at social gatherings, saying simply, "Today is my fast day." Fasting is also done for religious reasons. India's president, Narendra Modi, continued his annual nine-day "Navratri" fast even during his historic trip to America. This annual honoring of Divine Mother, and the triumph of good over evil, must have caused some head scratching during the state dinners.

It is now common medical knowledge that there are many important physical benefits to fasting. Among other things it detoxifies the cells, strengthens the immune system, controls blood sugar, and improves dietary habits. People also commonly use fasting to lose weight. The physical benefits are actually secondary, however, to the psychological and spiritual advantages.

Psychological benefits of fasting include strengthening one's will power and resetting poor eating habits, which seem to accumulate like burrs when we walk without awareness through life's fields. When we fast, we strongly declare, "I am in control here once again."

But the most important reasons for fasting are spiritual. Paramhansa Yogananda recommended that we fast one day per week and three days per month. He said fasting was one way to increase our spiritual magnetism, which he defined as "the power of the soul to attract or create whatever it needs for all-around happiness and well-being." Here are some other of his statements about the spiritual benefits of fasting:

"You, the soul, are far more than the perishable body of flesh. In fasting you discover that it is the cosmic energy, or *prana*, in the body that actually sustains you. Jesus pointed this out when he said, 'Man shall not live by bread alone, but by every word that proceedeth out of the mouth of God.' The 'mouth of God' is the subtle center in the medulla through which divine life energy, the 'Word,' flows into the body from its cosmic source."

"Fasting cleanses your blood and gives rest to your organs; a revitalized energy begins to flow through your eyes and hands and feet. Thus, when you are fasting you can transmit more healing energy to others when praying for them. As soon as you begin to realize you are living on cosmic energy and not on gross substances your body becomes magnetic."

As I said, I'm feeling much better after my day of fasting, and I don't mean only physically.

In joy,

Nayaswami Jyotish

WHERE HIS SHADOW FALLS

April 2, 2015

THERE ONCE WAS A MAN of such holiness and humility that he attracted the interest of the Heavenly Father. A messenger from God was sent to offer him any boon that he requested.

At first the saint could think of nothing to ask for, but then he said, "In my travels as a wandering monk, many people's paths cross my own. Grant me the gift that wherever I go, when my shadow falls on someone, he or she be healed or blessed. But, grant me also a further gift: May I never know."

I'm reading a remarkable book now, *Threads of Fate*, written by a friend of mine in Boston, Anna Shapiro. She tells the story of five generations of her family of Russian Jews: of the hardship, deprivation, and anti-Semitism they faced for more than a century in Russia.

But her story is remarkable not only for the difficulties they faced, but for its depiction of the indomitable strength, courage, tenacity, and deep spirituality of the human spirit.

In 1978, Anna and her family requested exit visas for America, knowing that it was unlikely they would receive them, and that they would be fired from their jobs as a result. For ten years their visas were denied, and, though highly educated, they survived only on subsistence work. Finally, in 1988, due to international pressure on behalf of Soviet Jews, the visas were granted, and they were able to emigrate to America.

Along her journey in Russia, Anna began studying and then teaching yoga, though at the time this was punishable by imprisonment. She also found a spiritual teacher, Joseph, who was a disciple of Paramhansa Yogananda. Then, in the mid-1980s, Anna made an important connection.

She writes: "Joseph told me that in America, in California, there was a center called Ananda, which in Sanskrit means, 'bliss.' This was a community of people living in the spirit of cooperation. One day

Joseph showed me Ananda's magazine in English. I asked him where he had gotten it, and he said: 'I cannot tell you.' He had translated all the articles word by word into Russian by himself, using a dictionary. Joseph also told me: 'You cannot imagine how much joy fills my heart when I read the Ananda Masters' articles about spiritual yoga.' And he added that this internal spiritual connection with Ananda gave him the strength to live, maintained his belief in God, and kept him consciously aware of the need for devotion to his chosen path—spiritual yoga.

"For me it was just an unbelievable dream to visit Ananda and meet with such spiritual people. I couldn't even imagine at that time that 14 years later I would be able to go there and enjoy meeting these wonderful people, some of whom became my friends."

In the mid-1980s I was part of the team that put together Ananda's quarterly magazine. Little did we know the blessings that were received where its shadow fell in distant Moscow, or that it would help Anna find her way to her spiritual family. God is the Doer.

In His love,

Nayaswami Devi

SAY "YES" TO LIFE

April 9, 2015

THE ANANDA COMMUNITIES MOVEMENT was born in the living room of Swami Kriyananda's small apartment in San Francisco. Most nights he travelled, teaching classes in various locations, but every Thursday evening he gave a satsang in his living room. Ten to twenty "regulars" formed the nucleus of what would, in time, become a worldwide movement.

A few months after I started coming to these satsangs in 1967, Swamiji offered everyone a chance to join him in his morning meditations. For one or two weeks a handful of people showed up. Then gradually the number dwindled until it was only the two of us. He eventually discontinued the meditations, but by then I was "hooked," serving as his helper and committed to a spiritual life. I've never understood why more people didn't take that opportunity.

Perhaps the most important element on the spiritual path is to accept the opportunities God offers us. So vital is this that Swami named his first album of songs *Say "YES" to Life!* Why should saying "yes" be so important? There are many reasons, but here are several that have been notable in my life:

• When I say "yes" I feel energetic and joyful and *everything* seems to go better. How could I take a single step forward without willingness?

• When I say "yes" I feel expansive, but when I begin to shut down I can get easily caught up in critical thoughts and negative emotions.

• God opens doors for us every day — watch carefully today and you'll see that this is true. Only by going through the first door does the next one open up. Eventually a whole pathway appears. As long as I stay with the flow I feel my footsteps are being guided.

• When I say "yes" to the inner promptings of my Guru, it deepens my connection.

• A resentful "yes" is like a "no" in disguise.

• When I say "no," it is not so much that doors shut, as that I fail to see any options, and I have a vague and foggy feeling that there should be something more to life.

• Sometimes I pull back out of the fear that if I say "yes," I will be overwhelmed. In fact, this rarely happens. Positive attitudes bring more energy, and then my days seem easy and fun. Mental resistance is what makes me feel overwhelmed. On the whole I've found it better habitually to accept whatever comes, and let Divine Mother take care of the details.

• Saying "yes" to little opportunities prepares me for the important ones—the ones that have determined the course of my future. It is probable that my life would have taken a different, less expansive, turn if I had never attended those Thursday satsangs and morning meditations with Swami Kriyananda.

• I can't always summon up the willingness to be affirmative. But as long as I do the best I can in the moment, I trust that God will bless my sincerity. As long as deep in my heart I seek Him, He reaches out His hand to help me.

When God asks something of you, the best advice I can offer is to echo the words of Sister Gyanamata, Paramhansa Yogananda's most advanced woman disciple, who said, "Say 'yes,' and make it snappy!"

In joy,

Nayaswami Jyotish

TWO BOWLS OF LEMONS

April 16, 2015

"Is there anything I can do to help?" I asked, as I entered the crowded kitchen at Ananda's Meditation Retreat. The staff was moving in high gear, busily preparing an elaborate Indian banquet for several hundred guests and residents to be served later that day.

With a grateful smile, the head cook pointed to a twenty-five-pound box of lemons, and said, "All those need to be juiced. Put them in a big bowl, and find a hand juicer [there was no electricity at the Retreat then]. You can go out on the deck and work there."

It was a beautiful summer's day, so I settled myself on the deck at a large table under a tree, and began the task at hand. I was happy to help in whatever way I could to prepare for the feast.

After a while, one of the guests saw that I was obviously enjoying myself, and asked, "Can I juice some lemons, too?"

"Sure," I replied. "Go to the kitchen, and get another big bowl and a hand juicer. We can work together."

He quickly returned, we divided the lemons into two bowls, and we began juicing away in the beautiful sunshine. After about five minutes, perhaps wondering why I seemed to be enjoying myself, my new friend said, "I think your lemons are better than mine." I willingly switched bowls so that he could work from mine, although I knew they were all from the same box.

Another five minutes passed, and he said, "I think your juicer is better than mine." Again I willingly switched, although I could see that there wasn't much difference between the two.

Another five minutes ticked away. Not finding this task very rewarding, the guest suddenly remembered, "Oh, I have something else I need to do now." I inwardly chuckled to myself as he departed, seeing that he hadn't found the secret of how to make it enjoyable.

Was there anything inherently fun in juicing the big bowl of lemons? Not really. As Paramhansa Yogananda said, "All conditions are neutral. It's what we think of them that makes them seem good or bad."

But I *was* enjoying myself because I brought enthusiasm, willingness, and joy to the task at hand. Whatever the day holds for you, try to approach it with an eager, positive attitude, and you'll find that life becomes filled with endless opportunities for joy.

In his book, *Affirmations for Self-Healing*, Swami Kriyananda wrote: "Enthusiasm is the spirit of joy channeled through the power of the will. To achieve happiness, one must work with happiness. To achieve divine joy, one must be keenly enthusiastic in everything one does!"

May you bring enthusiasm to even the simplest task that lies before you today, and may you learn how to turn all your lemons into lemonade.

With joy in God,

Nayaswami Devi

THE HAPPINESS CYCLE

April 23, 2015

PARAMHANSA YOGANANDA EXPLAINED that everyone in the world is driven by the same motivation: the desire to be happy and to avoid suffering. What makes life so complex is the variety of ways we chase happiness. There is a kind of Happiness Cycle that works like this:

1. We have a desire.

2. We act in an attempt to fulfill that desire.

3. If we succeed, we experience a period of happiness, but that happiness inevitably wanes. If we don't succeed, our desire is frustrated and can either flame into anger or become a vortex of subconscious longing that may cause us to reincarnate.

4. Either way, we experience suffering.

5. During those times that we aren't chasing a desire, we become bored. So . . .

6. We create another desire.

This endless cycle governs everything from fleeting desires that are fulfilled without our even being aware of them, to lifelong yearnings that cause us to be reborn over and over again. A momentary desire might be something like scratching an itch, while a lifetime one might be seeking to become rich or powerful. Eventually, before we can achieve spiritual freedom, all desires must end and be replaced by the single desire for union with God.

So often we're cautioned against being "worldly," but don't really understand what that means. It simply means that we seek our happiness "in the world," rather than within ourselves. The more we depend on something outside us, the more we become entangled and enslaved. That is why wise men warn us to resist the three great temptations: money, sex, and intoxicants. It is not that these things are evil in themselves, but rather that they are lures of maya and can easily become compulsions or obsessions.

Can we break this cycle? Yes! But only by realizing that fulfillment lies not in things, but is a state of mind. Desires ever fed are never dead. Can we simply decide, then, to be happy all the time? In theory yes, but in practice subconscious desires and old habits hold us back.

Spiritual freedom comes when we reverse the cycle that takes us outward. Try these steps:

1. Fill the mind with the desire for God.

2. Meditate, do sadhana, and practice His presence as much as possible.

3. As you feel His joy (true happiness), do your best to hold on to that experience.

4. The more we hold on to this ever-new joy, the more we will, as Patanjali tells us, "rest in our own true Self." In this state there is no longer any desire, boredom, or suffering.

To put it very simply: Don't chase after happiness. BE joyful.

In joy,

Nayaswami Jyotish

HOW TO BE A CHANNEL FOR GOD'S LIGHT

April 30, 2015

HELPLESS . . . hopeless . . . overwhelmed—it's easy to get drawn into these negative emotions when we see so much suffering in the world around us. Whether through natural disasters or man-made conflicts, the result is the same: we feel people's pain, but don't know how to help them.

But there is a way. I read a true story about a man who had a near-death experience after his car was crushed in a huge pile-up along a major freeway in America. At first, as his soul began to move upward above the wreckage, he experienced confusion and fear at having been precipitously thrust from his body.

Then he became aware of a beam of light coming from one of the cars that hadn't been damaged in the crash. His soul moved toward that light, and there he discovered a woman praying for others. As her prayers continued, the light expanded to touch the entire scene of suffering, and he felt great peace and comfort fill his soul.

Ascending into the astral world, the man was met by an angelic being who told him it wasn't yet time for him to leave his body. Later he regained consciousness and lived to tell the story of how someone's prayers brought comfort to those in need.

Swami Kriyananda gave us some beautiful suggestions on how to be a channel for God's light to relieve others' suffering:

God is happiest not in our efficiency, but in our increasingly humble attitude. Don't let thoughts of your own unworthiness hold you back from being a channel for God's presence. Self-forgetfulness and humility are the doorways through which God enters our consciousness and flows through us to others.

Serve joyfully, even in obscurity. Don't look to others for endorsement. Be content to seek the Lord's smile in your heart. In everything you do, try always to please God first. Whether or not others know about or appreciate your service is unimportant. Seeking their approval only puts the focus on you, and diminishes your ability to be a pure channel for the Divine.

Be centered in the inner Self. Don't let circumstances or people pull you down. Let God's light fill you when you work with others. Your inner Self is part of God, and remains ever untouched by any negative influences. No matter what happens, if you live in God's light and joy, you become filled with the strength to share His blessings with others.

Live more and more in that center where God dwells. Radiate this to others, and their lives, and your own, will be changed. Through the practice of meditation and attunement with the guru, you can move towards the divine center of all things, where God resides. When you turn your consciousness there, you increasingly become a sending station for His blessings, which alone can transform anything. Then your prayers, your thoughts, and even your touch can become channels through which God's light flows to help others.

Towards the One in All,

Nayaswami Devi

WHY DEVOTEES SUFFER

May 7, 2015

RECENTLY A FRIEND was sharing her story with us. Her long-term marriage had ended with the sudden death of her husband, and she was being tested on many levels at the same time. Her financial security had vanished, her health had deteriorated, and it seemed that her whole world was under attack. We could do little but listen quietly and send her our love.

Sometimes it's relatively easy to see why a person has drawn a karmic lesson: It's clear that they need to correct wrong attitudes and poor behaviors. But in this case, there seemed to be little apparent cause for such a level of challenge. She was a fine person, a longtime spiritual seeker who expressed a very uplifted consciousness, even during this tsunami of misfortune.

Over the years I've noticed a similar pattern in other sincere devotees, and have come to understand it in this way: When someone is close to finishing off their karma in a particular area, Divine Mother sends them an exaggerated test, which cauterizes the subconscious. The blow is so strong, and the lesson driven so deeply into the soul memory, that they never need to face that delusion again.

If we are ready, after countless lifetimes, to accept the fact that our strength and happiness come only from within, then we may attract the grace of having EVERYTHING taken away. Our non-attachment must be proven. When we are ready to offer ourselves unreservedly into God's light, we are a mere step from merging in Him.

To face squarely a powerful lesson, such as our friend was experiencing, takes great soul readiness. How do we prepare ourselves for something like this? In large part it is by being grateful for whatever comes our way. When a test comes, accept it, and cultivate the habit of asking that the lesson be complete. Sometimes we need to be a spiritual warrior and mentally say, "Bring it on, God, and let's finish this."

This is what Jesus Christ meant when he said, "But I say unto you, That ye resist not evil: but whosoever shall smite thee on thy right cheek, turn to him the other also. And if any man will sue thee at the law, and take away thy coat, let him have thy cloak also."

We are on the threshold of true wisdom when we understand that everything that comes to us is an expression of God's love. We are children who sometimes play with fire. If our Mother removes the flame to prevent us from being burned, let's not cry in outrage, but reach up our arms in childlike love. Then, as a beautiful chant promises, She will receive us on Her lap.

In loving acceptance,

Nayaswami Jyotish

DOING THE WORK

May 14, 2015

"KRIYA YOGA SAVED ME, just not in the way I thought it would." These intriguing words are from a letter we recently received from a friend. With her permission, we're sharing her experiences with you, because her insights are potentially life changing and something from which everyone can benefit.

The first thing our friend ever heard about meditation practices was someone saying: "Kriya will free you from every issue in your life." Having experienced a great deal of suffering since childhood, she took these words to heart and began her spiritual journey following Yoganandaji's path and Ananda.

But after some years of practicing Kriya, she found herself still struggling with many of the same problems that had plagued her all along. She wrote, "There is no doubt that I had grown spiritually as a result of my efforts and of God and Guruji's grace, but still, the issues were there waiting for me as soon as I got up from meditation."

Then after a period of seclusion two years ago, she had a life-changing insight that she still taps into today: "My mistake was thinking that the issues I have would dissolve without my having to do the work—that Kriya would do the work. Kriya has done the work, but not in the way I thought it would. It did not take away my pain and inner turmoil, or even change my behavior.

"What it did was to create a space of stillness within that allowed me to see my part in that pain and suffering, and thus my role in creating my life and my responsibility in changing it."

Then her inner transformation truly began.

What does "doing the work" mean? When we become aware of hidden mental and emotional patterns that cause us suffering, we need to exert the self-discipline to change them. God can show us what we need to change, but we need to put out the energy to break the self-created hold that delusion has on us.

This aspect of spiritual development is something that many devotees overlook, and yet it holds the secret to inner freedom. In *The Essence of the Bhagavad Gita*, Paramhansa Yogananda stated that achieving final liberation hinges on three simple thoughts:

1. Do you prefer happiness to suffering?

2. Are you willing to do the work to find lasting happiness?

3. Are you willing to renounce the ego?

When we can wholeheartedly answer "yes" to these questions, we walk the path to Cosmic Freedom.

With Master's joy,

Nayaswami Devi

THE POWER OF DIVINE LOVE

May 19, 2015

"SWAMI KRIYANANDA'S INFLUENCE will expand greatly now that he is no longer confined to a body. I have seen this happen with many other great souls." We were speaking with Sri D. R. Kaarthikeyan, one of the dignitaries who attended the dedication of the Moksha Mandir at Ananda Village this weekend. He speaks from experience, being an advisor to many spiritual works in India and throughout the world, as well as a dear friend of Swami Kriyananda. It seems that his prediction is already coming true.

It is Swami Kriyananda's birthday as I write this, and we just finished a three-hour meditation in the Moksha Mandir. This beautiful building (which somehow seems to be an amplifier for Swami's energy), the hundreds who attended, and Ananda itself are all testaments to Swamiji's love and expansion.

His love was most often expressed as divine friendship, and it touched the hearts of countless thousands around the world. This wave of kindness, in accordance with karmic law, came back to him in the form of friends everywhere wanting to show their gratitude. Day after day people arrived: more than six hundred from India and Italy, from Russia and Mexico and Argentina, and from other lands too numerous to list. Though languages varied, there were no strangers: We were united by our love for Swamiji, and by his for us. People smiled and laughed, chatted with each other, smiled and laughed, ate together, smiled and laughed . . . well, you get the idea.

This joy, too, was a gift from Swami Kriyananda, who was incapable of seeing anyone as a stranger, much less an enemy. He had a beautiful dream a few years before he passed, in which he saw myriads of people, good and bad, from all walks of life. When he awoke, in tears, he wrote down his experience on a little scrap of paper near his bed. This we have still, beneath an image of Master, on our altar. On it he wrote, "The more bliss I feel in myself, the more I find everyone around me utterly lovable. How vastly varied are the ways of approaching that same bliss!"

His ability to see everyone in their highest potential awakened something in the hearts and souls of all who knew him. And this weekend his divine friends gathered to honor him, to thank him, to dedicate his final resting place, and to bathe in his love. It was an extraordinary experience!

In divine friendship,

Nayaswami Jyotish

WHO IS IT THAT DIES?

May 28, 2015

DURING THE RECENT Dedication Weekend, May 15–17, we were meditating in Swami Kriyananda's newly completed Moksha Mandir, the final resting place for his body. His living reality was so tangible to everyone that it was hard to imagine he was no longer physically present with us. The difference now, perhaps, was that his consciousness felt even more powerful, accessible, and vast than before.

Two days later on the eve of his birthday, May 19, I had a vivid and meaningful dream. A small group of us were with Swamiji having tea in the comfortably decorated sitting room of a hotel. It seemed totally natural that we were together and enjoying the blessings of being with him.

Then another person joined us: Lila, who was Swamiji's devoted housekeeper and cook for twenty-five years, and who passed away nine months before him. Swamiji and all of us were surprised to see her, and marveled at the fact that she was with us, even though she was no longer alive.

When I awoke I realized that there was a difference in how I had experienced Swamiji and Lila in the dream. She seemed separated from us by a veil of energy, while he was vibrantly present, though neither of them still dwelt in physical form.

As I tried to understand why such a difference existed, I began to realize that this dream presented an important spiritual distinction for me to contemplate. Swamiji's consciousness, free from any vestige of ego, resided in timelessness. There is no past, present, or future in that state of awareness; nor life nor death, as we think of them.

Paramhansa Yogananda said, "When this 'I' shall die, then shall I know who am I." This freedom from all limitations of time and space is the goal that lies before all sincere spiritual seekers. The body will certainly die; the personality changes over time; with divine grace and inner effort, the ego can in time be transcended; but the soul remains unchanged eternally.

When we realize this, so much of the fear and anxiety over change, loss, and death leaves us, for we know who and what we really are. When faced with major changes in your life, or with the approach of death, whether your own or of a loved one, meditate on these words of Yoganandaji: "The reality of my life cannot die, for I am indestructible consciousness."

May we all discover our true Self in God.

In divine friendship,

Nayaswami Devi

NINE WAYS TO IMPROVE CONCENTRATION

June 4, 2015

"I REALLY WANT TO MEDITATE more deeply, but I have a hard time concentrating." This is a complaint we often hear from devotees. The mind seems to be programmed to be restless. A recent study by Microsoft showed that in the last thirteen years the length of time people can concentrate has decreased on average from 12 to 8 seconds. In fact, the study claimed that the typical person now has less ability to concentrate than a goldfish! This is partly due to the pace of life in modern times, and is made worse by media and social media consumption, technology, and multi-screening.

Obviously, meditation is not the only time people need to concentrate. Work demands it; family life demands it; and in fact we can't be a success in anything without concentration. Avoid multi-tasking: It is really only rapid shifts in concentration, and trains the mind to be restless. Do one thing at a time, do it with all your attention, and do it well. After you concentrate for a period of time, stop and take a rest.

It is a two-way street, of course: As better concentration helps our meditation, so too can meditation help develop our ability to concentrate. The need for concentration in worldly pursuits is an excellent reason for even worldly people to develop a meditation practice.

Here are nine ways to increase concentration during meditation:

1. Start your meditation with a strong determination to concentrate. If you don't consciously intend to concentrate, you won't. This means you must leave problems and plans outside your meditation room. Always begin with a prayer to God and Gurus. With their help everything is possible. Without their help, nothing is.

2. Begin with breathing techniques that calm the breath, and the mind will follow. A good way to start is with a few rounds of regular breathing: Inhale, hold, and exhale for the same count.

3. Tense and relax your body several times to overcome subconscious tensions. Then keep the body absolutely still. A friend of ours plays a mental game: "Nothing can make me move."

4. Bring your total focus to the point between the eyebrows, the center of stillness and concentration. Look into the light there. It is very helpful to visualize your guru, especially his eyes. If you are receptive, his God-consciousness will seep into your very soul.

5. Listen to the sound of AUM. It will help calm and center you.

6. When the mind wanders, bring it back. Do this quickly, before restlessness has a chance to build momentum.

7. Be patient. Concentration waxes and wanes. If you stay at it, your meditation will get deeper.

8. Engage the heart. With the deepest love possible, invite your guru to take charge of your life. If doubts or restless emotions try to grab you, burn them to ashes through the intensity of your devotion and a deep desire to be a channel of Divine Mother's love to everyone.

9. Paramhansa Yogananda said, "Chanting is half the battle." Chanting is a great help at the start of meditation to open the heart and focus the mind. It is also a way to refocus when the attention on deep meditation begins to fade. Here is a chant that helps deepen concentration. Meditate on the words; they are a lesson in themselves.

> Without meditation, mind, hither, thither wand'rest thou.
> Adorable Him! Search Him out in secret now.
> Floating on the breeze of bliss, in the chariot of sky,
> Peering into His eyes with thy diving eye,
> Thousand petals' nectar drink! Drink and drink, drink!
> With cosmic mighty Om, deeper do thou sink.

In divine friendship,

Nayaswami Jyotish

THE TRANSFORMING POWER OF GOD'S LIGHT WITHIN

June 11, 2015

As I sat in a meeting on that warm summer afternoon, I wasn't paying much attention to the crystals hanging in the window or to the faintly colored rainbows moving around the room. Those of us gathered were discussing some administrative matters for Ananda Village that I wasn't too involved in; my mind, I must admit, was elsewhere.

However, as the sun moved across the sky that afternoon, the light changed, and the rainbows suddenly became vibrant and beautiful. What was more, some of the rainbows rested right on the foreheads of those seated on the side of the room opposite the window. I don't know if others saw what I was seeing, because no one commented, but for me it transformed the whole experience.

Forgotten was the discussion of mundane matters, and before me sat radiant beings—noble and holy, with a diadem of rainbow colors on their forehead. Today, years later, I have no idea what the topic of discussion was, but I well remember the experience and the words that came into my mind at that moment—words that Yoganandaji had addressed to his disciples: "I see all of you as images of light. Everything—these trees, bushes, the grass you are standing on—all are made of that light. You have no idea how beautiful everything is!"

Recently I co-led a women's retreat at Ananda Village that was a transforming experience for all twenty-seven of us. At the end of the final morning we seated ourselves in a circle for a closing ceremony. Each of us in turn closed our eyes, offered up mentally our soul aspirations, and held aloft a lighted votive candle in a holder made of little hanging crystals. The woman seated to the left of that person then led us in this prayer: "Lord, bless the light that is in [person's name]." The rest of the group sent their love and blessings to her.

As the candle and prayers passed from person to person, at first tears quietly filled the eyes of the woman being blessed. Then some began to cry, and as we moved around the circle, one sobbed from a place deep within her heart.

At the conclusion, we all sat in silence for a while, very moved by what we had just experienced. I pondered what had caused such a powerful reaction. Eventually I realized that when we identify with our mistakes, shortcomings, and failures, we deny the true reality of our being. Then it becomes difficult and sometimes painful to accept that we are so much more, or to acknowledge the spiritual power of God's presence within.

When you become discouraged and see only darkness around you, try to remember these words of Yoganandaji: "I am submerged in Thy eternal light; it permeates every particle of my being. I am living in that light. Divine Spirit, I behold only Thee, within and without."

May you awaken to the light of God within.

In that light,

Nayaswami Devi

PREPARING FOR LIFE'S STORMS

June 18, 2015

WE HAVE BEEN READING a very interesting book: *Being Mortal,* by Atul Gawande. It's a thoughtful, well-written examination of aging and dying, subjects often ignored in modern society. Someday, perhaps, I will write a blog about that, but not today. This blog is about a small part of the process — about how helpful it is to prepare for difficulties before a crisis comes. For preparation makes a huge difference. How, then, can we prepare spiritually for life's storms?

We all have tests in life that are difficult, sometimes catastrophic. Over the years we have had the chance to see many people handle these trials, some with strength and grace, and others with hurt or bitterness. Here are some factors that make all the difference.

Acquire spiritual tools and learn how to use them. Just as every carpenter has a hammer and a saw, there are a few basic tools on the spiritual path that you should be using long before you need them in a crisis.

• A daily practice of meditation, the deeper the better

• A habit of filling the mind with positive thoughts and reactions

• A practice of listening to uplifting music, and mentally chanting throughout the day

• A sense of humor and the ability to laugh at life and at oneself

• A pattern of serving others. During a crisis you need to be a channel for positive energy. Otherwise the ego can turn inward toward self-pity and blame.

Develop a network of friends. People who feel connected to others have a safety net. In difficult times, especially, try to spend time with friends who are wise enough to help you see a bigger picture. Avoid, at such times particularly, those who pull your energy down or reinforce negative moods. If you feel a need to "vent," do so with someone centered and compassionate enough not to take your words too seriously.

Strengthen your own faith in God and Gurus. If you accept the simple truth that everything is an expression of God's love, you can go through any storm. Don't deny that challenges are happening, or even that they are difficult, but also don't accept them only on a surface level. An understanding that difficulties come to teach, not to punish, will mean the difference between soul freedom and egoic bondage. Meditate on the question, "What is this test trying to teach me?"

Learn to talk to God about little things. Paramhansa Yogananda said, "To those who think me near, I will be near." If, during the summer days, you have opened your heart and mind to God, then He will be waiting for you when winter arrives. As Yogananda says in his poem, "God! God! God!" "When boisterous storms of trials shriek, and when worries howl at me, I will drown their noises, loudly chanting: God! God! God!"

We cannot avoid life's storms, nor should we want to if we would grow strong. But we can prepare for them, and be ready to receive the light that always follows the darkness.

In joy,

Nayaswami Jyotish

IMITATING WHAT WE HEAR

June 25, 2015

T HE HIGH-PITCHED WHINE of the chain saw startled me, breaking the stillness of tall moss-covered cedars and lush green ferns. We'd been visiting the Ananda communities in Oregon and Washington, and now were enjoying a day on Camano Island off the coast of Seattle.

I'd been walking along absorbed in the forest's peace and quiet, which was accented only by an occasional bird song. Then as I came to a place where the trees were less dense, I first heard and then saw work crews high up on hoists limbing up trees to protect power lines.

The juxtaposition of the sounds of chain saws and birds' songs reminded me of a fascinating story. Biologists in the Amazon rainforest were studying what impact the destruction of the natural environment was having on animals there.

One day out in the field the biologists heard what sounded like a chain saw: the revving up of the motor as the saw was turned on, and the different pitches of whines as it cut through the trees. It turned out to be not a chain saw but a bird: the superb lyrebird, which has a tremendous gift of mimicry.

Perhaps to show that he was a versatile performer, the lyrebird also did a remarkable imitation of the click of a camera button and the soft whirring of its motor drive.

These were the sounds that it was hearing in its disappearing natural environment, and it was duplicating them with astonishing accuracy.

All life imitates what it hears—whether it's beautiful and uplifting or destructive and dissonant. When people express attitudes of hatred, racism, or religious bigotry, someone hears them. Perhaps it is a child who hears and imitates them as mindlessly as the bird mimicking the chain saw. Gradually, hatred and intolerance become hardwired into the child's mind, and, as in the rainforest, the natural environment of his soul qualities are destroyed.

As followers of the teachings of Paramhansa Yogananda, we need to sing his song of universal love and brotherhood so loudly that all can hear. Perhaps others, too, will join us in expressing his divine harmony, until people everywhere awaken from their dark dreams of hatred.

Here is one of my favorites prayers of Yoganandaji:

Prayer for a United World

"Let us pray in our hearts to establish a League of Souls and a United World. Though we may seem divided by race, creed, color, class, and political prejudices, still, as children of one God, we are able in our souls to feel brotherhood and world unity. . . . In our hearts we can all learn to be free from hate and selfishness. Let us pray for harmony among the nations, that they march hand in hand through the gate of a fair new civilization."

With a song of divine friendship,

Nayaswami Devi

JOY IS THE SOLUTION, NOT THE REWARD

July 2, 2015

IT WAS IN the late summer of 1967 that I first visited the land that was to become Ananda. August is hot in the foothills of the Sierra Mountains of Northern California, and we had spent all day working hard. I was part of a little group of Swami Kriyananda's students who had come to help him build Ananda's first structure, a small geodesic dome that was to serve as a temple.

At that time, Ananda communities were only a future dream for Swami. In this first year, he was simply trying to create a forest retreat where people could get away from their busy lives to learn and practice the teachings of Paramhansa Yogananda.

We had spent the day trying to erect the dome from thin wooden struts covered with plastic, but we were about to discover that the material we were using was too light for a building of this size. Just before sunset, the building began to sag, then suddenly collapsed at our feet in a pile of fragments. There was nothing to be done but have a light dinner, meditate, spread our sleeping bags out on the bare ground, and go to sleep.

In the morning I heard Swami murmuring to himself, and assumed that he was trying to come to terms with the disaster of the day before. But as I listened more closely, I could hear him repeating over and over, "Ah joy, ah joy!"

It had a profound effect on me, because at that moment I realized that Swami Kriyananda actually lived the truths he taught. Our moods *can* be under the control of our mind. Joy did *not* depend upon pleasant circumstances. Like the air we breathe, it simply was there, and we could choose to feel it or ignore it.

Some nine years later a fire destroyed virtually all the houses in our fledgling community. As one response, Swami Kriyananda and a merry band toured the United States on what we called the "Joy Tours": programs filled with music, classes, and laughter. A slogan used during those tours was, "Joy is the solution, not the reward." Again, it was a statement that we can choose to respond to misfortune either by expanding into joy or contracting into suffering.

The simple phrase, "Joy is the solution, not the reward," holds the key to a happy and successful life. Live with joy. Claim it as your divine birthright. Don't wait for anyone or anything to make you happy. If you cede that power to anything outside yourself, you also give it the right to make you *un*happy. Or worried. Or angry. Or everything else you don't want.

I learned a great lesson that summer morning in 1967, and again after the fire. Joy is a choice. It is something I try to choose at the end of each meditation and whenever I can throughout the day. When I do, I gain the power to smile at problems and laugh with life.

In joy,

Nayaswami Jyotish

WHY IS LIFE SUCH A STRUGGLE?

July 9, 2015

THE GARDENERS at Ananda Village's organic farm had very bad news to report that morning: "A frost has wiped out the tomato crop." "Insects are destroying the flower beds!" "Gophers have gotten into the carrots!!"

This was 1971. Our head gardener and farming mentor, Haanel Cassidy, was a vigorous man in his early seventies, who listened patiently to their tale of woe. Haanel had a lifetime of experience both in biodynamic gardening and as a disciple of Paramhansa Yogananda. Looking at the distressed faces of the young gardeners, he smiled ironically, and emphatically said, "Well, let's just quit!"

Of course, they knew this wasn't an option, and slowly they began to laugh. The gardeners learned an important lesson that day: Whatever obstacles lie in your path, face them head on, and be determined to find solutions.

I worked in Ananda's gardens for the first four years after I joined the community. Under Haanel's tutelage I learned a wealth about working with plants and the life force within them. But more importantly, I learned about life itself, for he was also a wise and loving friend to us young disciples.

One day, when I was going through a period of discouragement, I knocked at the door of his small geodesic dome, and asked if we could talk. We sat at his kitchen table, and I opened my heart to him about all the problems I was having and how discouraged I felt. He sat erect and still, listening quietly.

Finally I looked at him with tear-filled eyes, and asked, "Why does God make life so hard?"

He looked at me with wisdom and kindness born of experience, and answered, "There must be some value in the struggle itself." I've never forgotten his words—they've stood me in good stead through many difficult times in my life.

What is the value of the struggle? Surely it's to test our own inner strength, to prove our ability to overcome adversity, and to help us realize that there is an unseen, divine hand always reaching out to help us.

Haanel echoed the words of our guru, Paramhansa Yogananda: "Life is a struggle for joy all along the way. May I fight to win the battle on the very spot where I now am."

When the garden of your life becomes overrun with problems, don't quit, but fight. In the end, you'll discover your inner power and joy, and the presence of the Divine General who was always guiding you forward.

With joy in your victories,

Nayaswami Devi

GRATITUDE BRINGS HAPPINESS

July 16, 2015

Recently I received an email laced with unfair criticism, and my first reaction was to get defensive. I could feel my mind speeding up, getting ready to argue. Then I had a flash of insight and remembrance: You can't fight darkness with more darkness. I decided instead to neutralize negativity with gratitude. I thought about this person and recalled several things about him for which I was grateful. Within minutes my happiness level began to climb. I realized then that gratitude brings happiness.

Certain foods—leafy greens, vegetables, citrus fruits—cleanse and detox the body. Gratitude cleanses and removes toxins from the mind and heart. Gratitude, like fruits and vegetables, can be cultivated.

Try this: Each night before sleep, review your day and think of one person, one event, and one thing for which you are grateful. Vary this so you don't repeat anything for at least a week. This will train the mind to carry gratitude into the subconscious state. At first you may have to ignore, or even push away negative thoughts. Later you won't want them around any more than you would play with a rattlesnake.

Accept that life is full of challenges, and find a way to recast them in a positive light. In a letter, Paramhansa Yogananda wrote, "I used to come home, my hair saturated with smoke and my eyes burning after luncheon talks. I felt even suffocated. One day I made up my mind, Divine Spirit was smoke and light, and I was never bothered since. Mind is everything, whichever way you train it." Turning a light on or off takes the same amount of effort. Why not choose the light?

Gratitude is naturally expansive. When you feel circumstances trying to contract your heart into anger, judgment, or despair, push back with thankfulness. Try to do this immediately, when your instinctual reaction is to contract. This will help train new and brighter neural patterns.

You don't need to be perfect, but you do need to try. Little steps lead to long journeys.

The object of your gratitude matters only a little. What is important is the stream of thankfulness itself. That flow will warm the icy caverns that egotism has carved into your heart. Don't be afraid to recognize your foes and even give them names. It's hard to take your moods seriously when you say, "The Anger Gorilla is back again," or "The Ice Queen of Judgment is about to make a pronouncement."

Expand your heart: Take a moment and contemplate the web of people who make it possible for you to read this. There are those in the computer industry who design, manufacture, ship, and sell the device you are using. There are millions more involved in the trades that make your home or car possible. The chair you sit in has its own network of materials, production, roads, highways, and shipping that brought it to your doorstep. I could go on, but it is better if you do. Think in ever-widening circles of the incredible web that sustains you. Thank them, and most especially thank Divine Mother, who is, literally, the Mother of us all.

Gratitude will make you happy.

In gratitude,

Nayaswami Jyotish

DOES GOD LISTEN TO OUR PRAYERS?

July 23, 2015

"CONSIDERING THE VASTNESS of the universe, with its countless billions of galaxies, surely it is superstitious to believe that the Creator of this immensity listens to our prayers." A scientist once challenged Paramhansa Yogananda with these words.

The Master replied with profound wisdom, as well as gentle wit: "Your conception of Infinity is too finite! Although the Lord is infinitely vast, He is also infinitesimally small. He is as conscious of every human thought, every feeling, as He is of the movements of the vast galaxies."

Jesus Christ spoke a similar truth: "Are not two sparrows sold for a farthing? And one of them shall not fall on the ground without the knowledge of Our Father. Even the very hairs on your head are counted."

If God is watching the least little sparrow, why does it often feel that His attention is elsewhere when we need Him? In his beautiful book, *Whispers from Eternity*, Yogananda guides us on how to pray effectively to draw a divine response.

First, he suggests that we think of prayers not as beggarly petitions, but as *demands* that we can rightfully make because we are God's children. Then, he recommends these simple steps:

1. Calm your mind with a brief period of meditation.

2. Concentrate on a specific prayer-demand, and saturate it with devotion.

3. Feel that behind the screen of your devotional demand, God is listening to the silent words of your soul.

4. Remain concentrated and calm. You won't be able to focus your soul power if your mind becomes restless or agitated.

5. Believe absolutely that God has heard your prayer-demand.

Once we have done our best, we still need to understand that our prayers may not always be answered in the way we expect. Don't jump to the false conclusion that God hasn't heard you.

The challenges that we face in life are drawn by our own past actions — our karma. Why would God override the laws that He Himself has set in motion? As Omar Khayyam stated in his *Rubaiyat* (as paraphrased by Yogananda), "No amount of moral living, no theological hair-splitting, nor any piteous tears can erase a single one of them." So don't plead for amnesty from Divine Law, but demand deeper understanding as well as the strength to learn from and overcome all obstacles.

In the last analysis, the most important aspect of prayer is not the favors received, the problems removed, or even the understanding gained. It's simply learning to trust that God really is listening, and to speak to Him with complete openness and honesty. Once we realize that He's present for us eternally, we can live with an inner reassurance that everything in our life is, always was, and will continue to be held in the loving sight of God.

Your friend on the journey,

Nayaswami Devi

POSITIVE THINKING

July 30, 2015

Swami Kriyananda wrote an affirmation for positive thinking: "My outer life is a reflection of my inner thoughts. Filled with the joy of God, I express His joy and harmony in everything I do." This affirmation is so powerful that Devi and I repeat it daily, and have suggested that others from Ananda use it as a "theme" for the remainder of the year.

If our outer life really is determined by our thoughts, then it follows that changing our thoughts will change our life. Few people truly accept this reality, however. Most drift aimlessly or try to change the people and circumstances around them. They rarely stop to question whether that strategy actually works. If they spent a tenth as much time changing themselves, it would produce much greater gains.

The essential question, then, is *how* do we change our thoughts? The answer is simple in principle, but hard in practice. We must fight the battle for control between our negative and positive indwelling tendencies. Ultimately, the eternal soul must release itself from the compulsions of ego and the pull of the senses.

As Paramhansa Yogananda taught in his explanation of the Bhagavad Gita, the ego (represented by Bhishma) is supported by material desire (Duryodhana) and habit (Dronacharya). These major players are aided by countless other downward-pulling tendencies (the vast army of the materially minded Kauravas).

Arjuna, "devotee everyman" as Swami Kriyananda has called him, leads the fight for our positive aspirations. His allies are his brothers, who symbolize the spinal chakras, and Krishna (the guru). To win this war we must establish new patterns of thought and habit. Here are three things that I've found particularly helpful over the years.

Positive Thinking: We always have a choice between positive and negative thinking. The dice are loaded in favor of the negative due to the long tail of habit, so we need to train the mind to choose the light.

Affirmations: These form new habits of positive thinking. Say them out loud and then more and more softly, until you are repeating them mentally only but with deep conviction. Where the light dwells, no darkness can remain.

Chanting: Many chants are affirmations set to music, which makes their repetition more enjoyable and drives them deep into the subconsciousness. Choose a single chant that particularly appeals to you and repeat it over and over for several days or weeks. This will embed it so deeply that you will wake up with the chant ringing in your mind. One that I have been chanting lately is:

> Thou art my life. Thou art my love. Thou art the sweetness which I do seek.
> In the thought by my love brought I taste Thy Name, so sweet, so sweet.
> Devotee knows how sweet You are. He knows, whom You let know.

Remember, finally, that if you do your best to win this battle, God and Guru will drive your chariot to certain victory. Try, above all, to feel God's joy in meditation. Joy conquers all.

In joy,

Nayaswami Jyotish

GOD'S PROTECTING PRESENCE

August 6, 2015

"WOULD ANY OF YOU like to join me on a camping trip to Mt. Shasta?" With his characteristic enthusiasm and joy, Swami Kriyananda extended this invitation to a small group of us one morning. Swamiji had been asked to give a talk in nearby Shasta City and decided to combine this with a short vacation.

Mt. Shasta is a beautiful mountain in Northern California that majestically rises to 14,000 feet above the surrounding plains. Standing alone, Shasta is yet surrounded by many legends — stories of ascended masters living on, or even inside, the mountain. (Paramhansa Yogananda's comment was, "There are no masters living there." Then he added, intriguingly, "There *have* been colonists. However, no masters.")

We all accepted Swamiji's invitation, and Mt. Shasta's reputation for mystery didn't fail us. One morning as we were hiking up a trail leading to the summit, we noticed a few monarch butterflies floating down on the air currents. (We later learned that monarchs lay their eggs on the vegetation of Mt. Shasta. The annual emerging of the butterflies from their chrysalises coincided that year with the day of our hike.)

At first we were delighted to see these beautiful creatures floating around us, but as their numbers began to grow, our delight turned to dismay. We found it increasingly difficult to move through their dense clouds without damaging them.

Swamiji was in the lead, and as I looked ahead to see what we should do, I saw something remarkable: He was projecting an aura of light around him and our group, enabling us to walk forward as the thousands of butterflies parted around us. It was an unforgettable experience — one in stark contrast to another hike a few years later.

This time we were in San Francisco, where Swamiji was giving a series of classes during the summer of 1979. Upon the completion of his programs, he decided to celebrate with dinner and a movie, and invited those of us who had been helping to join him. As we left the theatre at the end of the film, a disturbing scene awaited us: It was late Saturday night, we were in a part of San Francisco filled with crime, and our cars were parked many blocks away.

Again Swamiji took the lead, but this time not through beautiful butterflies, but through drug sellers and suffering. With the same spiritual energy, he created an aura of light around us that simultaneously seemed to part the darkness and protect us. We arrived at the cars without incident. It was another experience that remains vivid in my memory.

As you move through life, you will sometimes find yourself in unexpected and bewildering situations. Whether surrounded by beauty and wonder, or by darkness and fear, consciously enfold yourself in God's light.

And remember these words of Paramhansa Yogananda: "Teach me to feel that I am enveloped always in the aureole of Thine all-protecting omnipresence: in birth, in sorrow, in joy, in activity, in meditation, in ignorance, in trials, in death, and in final emancipation."

With joy,

Nayaswami Devi

WHY WE NEED NATURE

August 13, 2015

A YOGI TOLD ME this story: "I was walking in the jungle with a companion when I tripped and accidentally gashed my leg very badly. Although we knew it would be dangerous to stay the night, I was unable to walk, and the situation looked bad. My companion, who had been trained as a healer, raised his hands and slowly began to turn in a circle. After some time he went to a tree, picked some leaves, and made a poultice. As soon as he applied it the bleeding stopped, and we were able to continue. He explained that he was unfamiliar with the herbs in that area and was asking the plants for help. The tree had offered its leaves and, if needed, would also have transferred its life-force to me." The yogi (Swami Gyanananda) concluded by showing me a faint scar that looked as if it were many years old, although only two weeks had passed.

This story is both true and a metaphor for our relationship with nature. Our lives depend upon the other inhabitants of our planet. They give us the oxygen we breathe, the food we eat, and the medicines with which we heal. There are more microbes in a single teaspoon of soil than there are humans on the earth. Scientists have discovered that even our bodies are not only our own: they contain a microbiome with ten times as many cells from microbes as from human cells. Life is not possible without this symbiotic relationship.

There is also, beyond the merely physical, a connection of consciousness, which we can deepen if we choose. The great American botanist, George Washington Carver, said, "Everything in nature will speak to you, if you love it enough." Among many others, J.C. Bose, the great Indian scientist, has demonstrated that awareness continues not only into the animal and plant worlds, but into the mineral as well. These subtle and profound connections form a great web of consciousness.

Studies show that hospital patients heal more quickly and need less medication if they have a window that looks out on nature. Even a photo or painting of a tree can ease pain, lower blood pressure, and quicken healing. Sociologists have shown also that increasing the number of trees in a city results in a lowering of crime. When we cooperate with nature, it cooperates with us. But too often nature is subjugated or destroyed due to man's indifference or greed, and, in our isolation from the natural world, we end up breeding disease and unhappiness.

There is also a more spiritual dimension: When we feel a loving connection with the nonverbal world of plants, animals, and minerals, we open hidden recesses in our own consciousness. Communication with nature is best done in quietness of body and mind, through feelings or word pictures. This type of nonverbal stillness is also needed for deep meditation. Inner stillness comes when we calm the body and mind through the techniques of yoga or by withdrawing the life-force through pranayama. Only then, when we move beyond our incessant mental chatter and restlessness, can we become aware of the unmoving presence of God. Then we will know that we are part of all that is.

In divine friendship,

Nayaswami Jyotish

IS IT POSSIBLE TO FAIL SPIRITUALLY?

August 20, 2015

"WILL I EVER LEAVE the spiritual path?" a disciple of Paramhansa Yogananda once asked him. "How could you?" the Master replied. "Everyone in the world is on the spiritual path."

In the broadest possible terms this statement is true, because everyone is striving to find happiness and avoid suffering. The main difference between a truth-seeker and a materially minded person is where they look for their happiness: within or without.

The questioning disciple eventually did leave the ashram. Perhaps the Master foresaw this and was consoling him for what lay ahead. In any case, the question is an important one for us: *How do we fail spiritually, and can it be avoided?*

Take Small Steps with Joy

We heard a story told by a well-known track coach who worked with world-class athletes. He noticed that when these runners would be one-hundredth of a second over their record time, they would be upset for the entire day.

One day, a group of elderly librarians asked him, "Will you help us get started with an exercise program?" He suggested that they begin by walking around the track. To his surprise, they were utterly delighted by being able to walk a quarter of the way. Realizing he had been working with the wrong people, he began training those who found joy in the smallest accomplishments.

To succeed spiritually, try to see the path as a joyous journey, not an impossibly steep ascent. Meditate not *for* joy, but *with* joy. Set goals for yourself that you can meet, and move forward step by step to freedom.

Trust Your Own Sincerity

A devotee once said to Swami Kriyananda, "I feel insincere when I sing the chant 'I Want Only Thee, Lord,' because I know that there are still many things other than God that I want." Swamiji replied, "Try inwardly chanting, 'I *want* to want only Thee, Lord.' In this at least, you are sincere."

We are a house divided: Part of us knows that happiness lies within, but another still seeks fulfillment in the world. Don't let your lower tendencies convince you that you are a half-baked devotee, or discourage you from seeking God. Define yourself by your aspirations rather than by your present state, and hold firmly to the thought, "*I may have stumbled along the way, but my intentions are sincere.*"

"Give Me Thy Failure"

Finally, these words from the Bhagavad Gita provide the best answer to our question, "How can we avoid spiritual failure?":

Clasp Me with heart and mind! so shalt thou dwell
Surely with Me on high. But if thy thought
Droops from such height, despair not!
Give Me lower service! seek to reach Me, worshipping
    with steadfast will;
And, if thou canst not worship steadfastly,
Work for Me, toil in works pleasing to Me!
For he that laboureth right for love of Me
Shall finally attain! But, if in this
Thy faint heart fails,
Bring Me thy failure!

If God accepts even this, how can we possibly fail?

With joy,
Nayaswami Devi

TWO QUESTIONS

August 27, 2015

N EARLY THIRTY YEARS AGO a member of Ananda, Dr. Peter Van Houten, started a medical clinic, which has grown over the years to now serve over 5,000 people. People coming to the clinic often hope for a quick fix, a shot or pill to make them well or at least ease their symptoms. The clinic is in a relatively poor rural area and many of the patients smoke, drink, and use drugs. Dr. Peter knows that he will see these same patients again. And again. And again.

Spiritual teachers and counselors face variations on the same theme. Rather than physical health, people are generally seeking help with relationships, work issues, or life directions. When dealing with these issues people ask, sometimes obliquely, for approaches on how to get their partners or co-workers to change their conduct and be more harmonious. Until they ask for insights about their own behavior, however, it is likely that they, too, will return again and again.

Both of these groups suffer from the same fundamental mistake (which is the basic delusion of maya) that makes them think that happiness can be obtained by changing something outside themselves. People with habitual behavioral problems rarely ask the two most important questions.

The first question is: What do I need to change *in myself?* It is not easy to get people to see that their outer life is a projection of their inner consciousness. And yet, as long as their consciousness stays the same, they will magnetically attract the same issues and karmic patterns again and again. A statement that has been attributed to Einstein is, "You cannot solve a problem from the same consciousness that created it. You must learn to see the world anew."

Many people develop strong defenses to avoid looking at their own part in their chronic issues. Others feel guilty or have low self-esteem, but this doesn't help either. It is better not to say, "I am bad," but rather to say, "I have some patterns that need to change."

The second vital question is: *How* can I raise my consciousness?

Healing can truly begin only when one not only accepts the need to change but also asks *what changes* are needed. It is usually better to look for directional changes rather than specific ones. That is, think first of how to change your energy patterns and only secondarily of the specific form the resulting changes will take. A dieter should think of how to change eating behaviors rather than just modify specific foods. Once we realize that outer circumstances and behaviors are created by inner thoughts, we are on the right track.

Paramhansa Yogananda made a very important statement about changing ignorant behavior. "Sin," he said, "is not like dynamite, which you can explode from a distance without harm to yourself. It has to be defused within your own soul." When we still our energy and uplift our minds, hearts, and souls by meditation, service, and good environment our problems will begin to evaporate.

In divine friendship,

Nayaswami Jyotish

THE YOGIC LIFESTYLE

September 3, 2015

"CAN THE PRACTICE of yoga help me in daily life?" New students, looking for practical solutions to their problems, often ask this question.

The science of yoga is India's unique contribution to the upliftment of human consciousness. Not affected by passing time or different cultures, yoga remains a timeless, universal body of teachings available for the benefit of everyone.

Yet yoga is more than the specific practices done in the isolation of an ashram or meditation room. It also offers attitudes and practical applications that taken together form an effective, fulfilling approach to life: the yogic lifestyle. Let's look at three aspects of it.

Yoga Means "Union"

To succeed at anything in life, or to understand things at their heart, we need to concentrate and become absorbed in them. Whether in artistic expression, scientific inquiry, or any field of endeavor, when we focus and become immersed in what we are doing, something magical takes place: we forget ourselves and experience a sense of expansion that transcends our personal reality. We then can pierce to the heart of any problem before us.

In fact, in the classical teachings of yoga as presented by Patanjali, this process is described as the last three steps of *ashtanga yoga*, or the eightfold path: *dharana*, or concentration; *dhyana*, or absorption; and *samadhi*, or bliss.

Paramhansa Yogananda said that scientists study the atom, but yogis *become* the atom. In our daily lives, success and happiness rest on one of the foundation stones of the yogic lifestyle: become one with what you are doing.

Yoga Is a Science

The scientific method has shown us the value of presenting a theory, and then testing its validity through experimentation. This approach can be applied to our own life. Yoga says that meditation brings peace of mind: Try for yourself and see if this is true. Yoga says that right attitudes such as non-violence, honesty, and generosity bring happiness: Test this out in the cold light of day, and see the results.

Once you've experimented and proven to yourself the efficacy of these teachings, no one needs to convince you of their value. The yogic lifestyle embodies a courageous approach to finding truth and self-discovery.

Yoga Awakens Us to Our Place in a Greater Reality

Through the practices of yoga, fears and anxieties are lifted from our heart, and we can experience a greater reality, of which we are just a small part. Worries begin to fade away and are replaced by a wonderful reassurance that everything in life comes from a benevolent, omnipresent consciousness.

In the beautiful words of my Guru, Paramhansa Yogananda: "While millions are thinking they are approaching old age, death, and oblivion, we know we are approaching eternal life, eternal youth, eternal wisdom, and eternal protection."

Swami Kriyananda has said that the Ananda communities are living laboratories for the benefits of yoga in daily life. Try it for yourself and see.

With joy in self-discovery,

Nayaswami Devi

SPIRITUAL BIRTH

September 10, 2015

SEPTEMBER 12TH IS the anniversary of the day in 1948 when Swami Kriyananda first met Paramhansa Yogananda. Those of us who are members of Ananda consider this day as our collective "Spiritual Birthday." Devi and I are in Italy and will celebrate this sacred occasion by giving a talk to several hundred people at a Yoga Festival in Rome.

I won't recount the story of how the then Donald Walters came to find himself kneeling at his guru's feet. That is beautifully told in *The New Path*. On that Sunday afternoon Yogananda asked two questions of this new disciple: First, "I give you my unconditional love. Will you give me your unconditional love?" "Yes!" replied Swami.

And then, "And will you also give me your unconditional obedience?"

The young seeker wanted to be absolutely sincere in his answer, so this second question posed a greater challenge. "Suppose sometime I think you're wrong?" he asked. Master replied, "I will never ask anything of you that God does not tell me to ask." Then, with great determination, Swami replied, "Yes."

Swami's answers were on behalf of all of us. He was at that time "devotee everyman," as he once described Arjuna's role in the Bhagavad Gita. These two questions all disciples must answer for themselves. Until we can sincerely answer, "Yes!" we will but meander along the spiritual path.

Few of us will ever kneel in front of a Self-realized master, but each of us must kneel in front of God. He has already given us His unconditional love—we could not take a single breath nor live a single second without it. But He has given us the free will to withhold our love from Him. How many lifetimes we have wandered through the barren desert of life seeking that love from dry creeks. We have a God-shaped hole in our hearts, which can never be filled until we finally accept His love and offer ours in return.

We must also be ready to accept some form of discipline, of obedience to the will of God. We may think we have free will, but it is circumscribed by past karma. As Yogananda said on that occasion, "In the beginning of the spiritual path, one's will is guided by whims and fancies. . . . If you attune your will to mine, you too will find freedom." When we are truly ready to travel the path to Self-realization, we need the guidance of someone who knows its winding ways.

May I suggest that, on this sacred occasion, you meditate deeply and, before God, in the silence and sincerity of your heart, ponder these same two questions? Your answers are, perhaps, the most important ones you will ever be asked to give. Your life—or lives—depends upon your answer.

In divine love,

Nayaswami Jyotish

WHEN GOD SPEAKS

September 17, 2015

THE TROUBLED YOUNG MAN knelt amidst the crumbling ruins of the chapel and prayed. A few years earlier he had been a carefree youth who enjoyed partying with his friends. Then a war came, and he joined the army looking for adventure. Captured in one of the battles, he was held prisoner for a year and suffered from recurring high fevers.

Finally the sick young man was released, and after a long period of recuperation he emerged a changed person. No longer interested in partying, he became silent and solitary, desperately seeking to find the purpose of his life.

Wandering the hillsides near his home, he found a small abandoned chapel and knelt in prayer before a painted wooden crucifix. So deep and sincere were his prayers that the image of Christ became a living reality and spoke to him: "Rebuild my church," Jesus said, "which has fallen into ruin." The year was 1205, and that man is known today as St. Francis of Assisi.

For the past month we've been visiting our community near Assisi, and a few days ago we went to San Damiano, the little chapel where St. Francis heard Christ speak and began his mission. We, too, prayed here, and although eight hundred years have passed since Christ appeared to Francis, the deep interiorized power of his experience still lingers.

As Paramhansa Yogananda explains, the Christ consciousness, the conscious presence of God in creation, exists everywhere at all times. But when we call to Him with deep intensity and devotion, God speaks to us in the form we worship.

A friend living at Ananda Assisi shared with us a story, similar to that of St. Francis, of how God spoke to her. The experience took place when she was fifteen years old and living in the town of Calabria in southern Italy. Every year on a certain date there is a procession in which a large statue of the Madonna is carried through the streets of the town, and then returned to the church.

At the end of the procession, our friend knelt before the Madonna, who became a living presence and spoke to her, saying "You are the only one who has come to see Me."

"But, Holy Mother," she replied, "the church is filled with people."

"Yes, My child," the Madonna said, "but you are the only one who has come to see *Me*. The others have come to be seen." The Divine Mother then asked her to build a shrine in a specific area outside of town, which, after much difficulty and several miracles, she was able to do.

God speaks when we converse in His language: utter, selfless love. In his poem, "Breathe in Me," Yoganandaji wrote:

> You may hide behind the ocean,
> You may hide behind delusion,
> You may hide behind life, . . .
> But you cannot hide behind my love,
> For in the mirroring light of my love
> You are revealed.

May we all know such love,
Nayaswami Devi

THE ONE PERCENT SOLUTION

September 24, 2015

THIS MORNING DEVI AND I spoke with someone who was feeling overwhelmed and a little guilty because he couldn't keep up with all the "should do's" on the spiritual path. I doubt if there is a devotee alive who hasn't had these same thoughts. On the one hand, there are hundreds of techniques, habits, and attitudes that could be helpful. On the other hand, we have to face the reality of living in this world with multiple responsibilities and limited time.

Paramhansa Yogananda presented us with a great variety of teachings and techniques. Because of his great magnetism and enthusiasm, they all seem to be good, and many essential in the quest for Self-realization. Yet he also said, "If you do one one-hundredth of what I suggest, you will find God." This is so reassuring. It keeps us from feeling so inundated or overwhelmed that we just give up.

A friend recently shared something that can help us keep moving ahead. He said that some years ago the British national cycling team wanted to improve their world ranking. They hoped to become the top team within five years. The coach came upon this solution: We will improve everything we do by at least one percent. They looked at their equipment: bikes, wheels, helmets, and other gear. They reexamined their training, diet, and even got better pillows. They revised their racing strategies, and . . . well, you get the point. They did not achieve the goal of being the best in the world in five years. It took them only three.

If we apply this strategy to our spiritual practices, it will yield great results. First try to optimize some easily changed physical areas such as your meditation room, altar, meditation seat, malas, and other equipment. Improving some of these things may take very little effort and, once done, won't need more attention. Try to improve every little thing you can think of by at least one percent.

Then move on to important habits such as regular meditation times and length, good posture, diaphragmatic breathing, starting each meditation with deep relaxation and concentration, and ending with a sense of expansion and joy. These may take more effort to improve, and will need to be revisited regularly. But, here again, if success is judged by making only small improvements, it can be accomplished relatively easily.

Finally, let's look at the really important things: deep devotion, faith, non-attachment, and surrender of self-will to God's will. These are the areas that bring Self-realization. They are also places where the 1% solution can make a big difference. If we just keep taking a step at a time we will eventually arrive at our goal. As the great householder avatar Lahiri Mahasaya said, *"Banat, banat, ban jai!* Doing, doing, one day done!"*

In celebration of little steps,

Nayaswami Jyotish

THE BROKEN CONNECTION

October 1, 2015

"DOCTOR, PLEASE HELP ME. I think that I'm really sick," the worried patient said. "My body hurts all over: when I touch my arm, it hurts; when I touch my chest, it hurts; when I touch my head, it hurts."

After running a battery of tests, the doctor reported to his patient, "I've got good news and bad news. The good news is there is absolutely nothing wrong with your body. The bad news is you have a broken finger, so wherever you touch, it hurts!"

An Indian friend recently told us this story, and though we laughed at the punch line, there is also a deeper message in it. When our consciousness is filled with awareness of our union with God, it's like a happy, healthy body. The broken finger is like the ego, which breaks our connection with a greater reality, and makes us imagine suffering everywhere, when in reality all that hurts, all that is "broken," is the little self.

Think of it this way. The ego is merely the soul identified with the body and personality. Like blinders on a horse, the ego confines our field of vision to a narrow part of the world around it. Take off the blinders of ego and our awareness grows much broader. Then, as we begin to see things from a God's-eye view, the world becomes filled with beauty and joy.

In a storm, the surface of the ocean knows no peace. Similarly, as long as the storm of ego rages in the mind, a person knows tension and anxiety. As the waves of ego diminish, the devotee relaxes and accepts once again his connection with the peace and happiness of the infinite Spirit.

How do we diminish the hold of the ego and reestablish our divine connection? Swami Kriyananda put it clearly and simply: "Finding God is easy. It's a matter of two things: longer, deeper meditations, and seeing God as the Doer in all things."

The broken connection is caused by our ego asserting its independent reality from God. This keeps us forever trapped in the world of suffering and uncertainty. Meditation and surrender of the little self open the door of our soul to true happiness and freedom.

As Paramhansa Yoganandaji said, "With God, life is a feast of happiness, but without Him it is a nest of troubles, pains, and disappointments."

Let's strive to heal our broken connection with God, so that everything we see, touch, or hear fills us with His joy.

At His feet,

Nayaswami Devi

FINDING *AUTOBIOGRAPHY OF A YOGI*

October 8, 2015

IT WAS IN THE FALL of 1966 that I found *Autobiography of a Yogi*, although in truth I think it found me. It was a time of great transition in my life. I had graduated from college and moved to San Francisco a few months earlier, and was just starting out as an independent adult. I was looking for a direction, having felt that my major in college, psychology, was simply not capable of answering the questions I had long been asking. I was interested in awareness, in the scope of human consciousness, and in happiness. More schooling was not going to give me what I was seeking. And yet, where was I to turn? I had long abandoned religion, at least the formalized "Churchianity" I was given in my youth.

San Francisco was an amazing place in 1966. While I was not into the hippie scene, there was a palpable sense that new paradigms were possible. The treadmill of school, job, marriage, family, career, and death seemed to be more and more distasteful, not only to me but to thousands of others as well. And yet, rejecting old ways did not automatically produce new answers. The question of how to find a meaningful life was becoming urgent. Then, the *Autobiography of a Yogi* found me.

I was 23 years old when my brother-in-law gave me a copy. As I began to read, a whole new world opened before me. Here was someone talking about the vast potential of consciousness, not from theory, but from experience. Here was a spirituality that was alive, dynamic, practical, and part of everyday life rather than prayers repeated on Sunday morning like formulas, then forgotten for the rest of the week. I was overwhelmed by gratitude to be shown a world with real meaning and purpose. It felt as if my narrow, overly rational world had begun to unravel like a threadbare sweater when the stitching fails.

As I read on, there were many things I could not fully accept.

Many of the miracles were simply beyond me, having no part of the "reality" of a small town in Minnesota, where I'd grown up. But I utterly accepted the author's integrity. I knew in my bones that Paramhansa Yogananda was speaking the truth from experience and realization. Those things that I couldn't yet accept, I was able to put on a mental shelf, rather than reject them outright.

I felt transformed by reading the book, but I had no idea what to do next. So I continued to read similar types of books: Zen Buddhism, the *Tibetan Book of the Dead*, even some American Indian spiritual teachings. But none of them resonated like the *Autobiography*. A few months later I met Swami Kriyananda and my life direction took a whole new turn.

My brother-in-law was given Kriyananda's address in San Francisco, and we were eager to meet this direct disciple of Yogananda. It was Easter Sunday, April 26, 1967, when we knocked on the door of his modest second-story apartment; he greeted us, and we exchanged names. Then he said, "I'm working on a project. Do you want to help?" We readily agreed. The project was to address envelopes for a mailing about upcoming classes, but I've often joked that I said "yes" to a project that is still continuing some 48 years later.

In gratitude,

Nayaswami Jyotish

FIVE DAYS IN THE TIMELESS ZONE

October 15, 2015

"WE'LL NEVER GET all this work done by the end of the week," I lamented to Jyotish. In 1982 Swami Kriyananda had asked us to lead Yoga Teachers Training, which was held at the Meditation Retreat. Because we'd need to be available for the students, we realized it was necessary to move to the Retreat—six miles away from our home at Ananda Village.

After looking at the few available houses that might work for us and our eight-year-old son, we decided that the best option would be to renovate Swamiji's original dome-home. His dome hadn't been regularly used for several years after Swamiji moved to his residence at the Village, Crystal Hermitage, and was in serious need of restoration.

We had five days to make whatever changes we could, leaving us a few days to prepare for the three-month-long course about to begin. This was cutting it very close indeed.

Jyotish had some experience in building domes, and he evaluated what needed to be done: "First, we'll need to clean the interior and remove all the styrofoam triangles that form the inside walls. Then we'll have to insulate, and cut new triangles out of sheetrock (about 60 equilateral triangles four feet on a side). These will need to be nailed into place to form pentagons and hexagons, and all the seams taped. The next step is to plaster and texture the interior to create a unified surface. Finally, after that dries, we can paint it."

Thus, my lament: in five days? With just the two of us doing the work?

Nevertheless, we set a project schedule with daily goals and began work on Monday morning. By noon when we took a meditation break, we looked at what had been accomplished, and saw that we'd completed only about one-tenth of our goal for the day. Picking up after lunch, we didn't have much hope of finishing, but all we could do was to keep going.

Then something remarkable happened. We continued working in the same way with no extra help, but somehow we slipped into a different flow. The work seemed to happen effortlessly, not in a normal pace of time, but in a "timeless" zone. By six o'clock that evening, we'd completed the day's goal.

The same thing happened the next day: by noon only a small fraction of the job was done, but by the end of the day it was finished. In this way, we arrived at Friday afternoon and realized with amazement and gratitude that the whole project was done. And it was beautiful!

Krishna's words from the Bhagavad Gita came to mind: "To those who worship Me, I make good their deficiencies and render permanent their gains."

Whatever our goal — whether renovating a house or achieving liberation — if we do it step by step with the thought of God, and don't worry about the enormity of the job before us, the seemingly impossible can happen.

With heart's gratitude,

Nayaswami Devi

MAGNETIZING YOUR LIFE

October 22, 2015

WE HAVE BEEN HELPING give a Meditation Teacher Training course here in India, and, as part of the training, we talked about how to give magnetic classes. But the same principles apply to other areas of life: doing your job with magnetism, or having magnetic relationships, or developing the magnetism that draws God. Magnetism, you see, is produced whenever there is a flow of energy. It follows a basic law stated by Paramhansa Yogananda: "The greater the will, the greater the flow of energy. And the greater the flow of energy, the greater the magnetism." It is not too simplistic to say that this is also the law of success in any endeavor.

One of Swami Kriyananda's first music recordings was called, "Say 'YES' to Life!" Saying "yes" enthusiastically is the best way to increase your energy. Whatever we do with enthusiasm will be magnetic, which is why we always see dynamic energy in magnetic people. A second trait of successful people is high focus or concentration of energy. In many cases of true genius, the focus reaches such levels of concentration that they're unaware of the need to eat or even to sleep until their project is done. On a very minor scale, sometimes when I am concentrating on painting a picture, I will become aware, some hours later, of the fact that my legs have been asleep. So, we have two key elements, enthusiasm and focus.

But we also have to remove the impediments to the flow of energy. Here is an example: Fiber optic cables are made of hair-thin strands of ultra-pure glass. A laser pulse can travel over a hundred miles through one of those strands before it must again be amplified. There are two critical factors both of which are also important to a successful life. The first is that the glass must be as pure as possible. Any distortions or impurities will block or deflect the flow of photons. In us, these impediments are things like pride, or lack of confidence, or negativity, or, in fact, any egocentric thoughts. The reason we enjoy movies or sports is because we focus deeply and forget ourselves.

The second vital element in a fiber optic cable is a mirror-like covering, which keeps the photons from straying off course. For us this means we must learn to redirect our thoughts back to the task at hand. A good tool for this is to set a kitchen timer for a period of uninterrupted concentration. While it is running, don't multitask, don't space out, keep your mind focused. Just do what you need to do.

So here is the simple formula:

1. Be enthusiastic about whatever you are doing.

2. Forget yourself and focus on the task alone.

3. If your mind wanders, bring it back. And

4. Stay with one thing until you finish it.

Does this sound like the same advice we would give to someone trying to deepen his meditations? Yes, of course. Our spiritual life and our everyday routines are cut of the same cloth. It is all God's light.

With joy,

Nayaswami Jyotish

HOW TO DEFEND A PRINCIPLE

October 29, 2015

SWAMI KRIYANANDA INVITED US over for tea one afternoon to discuss a change he had in mind for Ananda. When he asked our thoughts, I responded with some emotion, because I felt that a principle was at stake. Swamiji looked at me steadily and said, "You may be right, but when you speak so emotionally, it's hard to accept what you're saying."

A little while later another person joined us, and Swamiji asked her to consider the same question. Though she came to the same conclusion that I'd expressed, her words were reflective and calm. To her, Swamiji said, "I accept your perspective as the right course to take."

This was a very good lesson for me: True principles are powerful because they are rooted in impersonal truth. Defending them with an emotional reaction only clouds their essence and weakens their impact.

Recently I found these words from Kriyanandaji's *Living Wisely, Living Well*: "If you feel impelled to defend a principle, never do so under the influence of anger. Defend your beliefs joyously! *Dharmic*—which is to say, righteous—causes should be defended righteously. And joyous non-attachment is the only way to mount that defense."

One of my favorite stories about how to defend principles is from the life of one of the early Christian fathers, St. Anthony. He lived alone in the deserts of Egypt, praying and meditating in isolated caves for many years. At the same time, a religious controversy began to brew in the emerging Christian church, threatening to destroy it.

The schism centered around two opposing views of Jesus Christ. One side held that he was a divine incarnation, an enlightened being. The other averred that he was a wise teacher, but not of an exalted spiritual stature. Emotionally charged debates filled the big church in Alexandria, causing increasing confusion in the minds of Christ's followers.

Finally, in desperation, some young monks sought out Anthony in the desert and begged him to settle the debate. Reluctantly he returned to be among men, and quietly entered the back of the church where the debate was raging. So great was his spiritual presence that one by one everyone turned to look at him, and the angry voices became silent.

Though he was unaccustomed to speech, he uttered four words that changed the course of Christianity. Anthony simply said, "I have seen Him," then quietly slipped away. In those few words, St. Anthony was able to convey his personal experience of Christ's divinity in such a way that no reasoned argument could ever do. The debate was over, and Christ was recognized as an incarnation of God Himself.

If you believe in something, whether a divine being or a principle, become one with it in your heart. When words are needed to defend it, you will have the inner power to uphold the truth.

Your friend in God,

Nayaswami Devi

THE MOST MEMORABLE TALK

November 5, 2015

W E'RE IN INDIA and recently had lunch with Indu Bhan, whom you may remember as the man who told us the fascinating story of how he and his companions found Babaji's Cave. Indu is a font of amazing and inspiring stories, and he asked us if we would like to hear about the most memorable talk he had ever attended. Seeing the twinkle in his eye, we were eager to hear the tale.

"I had to pay a small amount to attend," he began. "First there were fifteen minutes of kirtan, or devotional chanting. Then the teacher came on stage and said, 'Everything that happens to you is a blessing from the Divine meant for your spiritual evolution.' Then he walked off!

"Another fifteen minutes of kirtan ensued, and again he came on stage and repeated, 'Everything that happens to you is a blessing from the Divine meant for your spiritual evolution,' and walked off a second time. Another fifteen minutes of kirtan, and out he came again and repeated the very same sentence. Then he left, and that was the end of the evening."

Indu concluded by saying that even though he was a youth at the time, and many decades have passed, he has never forgotten the evening or the talk.

Devi and I are practicing this lesson in our own way. We've been in the Himalayas helping to lead two consecutive weekend pilgrimages to Babaji's Cave. In the intervening week, we were also fortunate to take seclusion at a retreat near Lohaghat, and visit some other sacred spots associated with our line of gurus. During this period we are accepting everything, every detail, as a blessing from the Divine in the form of Babaji.

Some remarkable things happened on the pilgrimages. There were several people who felt that their being able to come at all was a miracle in itself. One had been having dizzy spells and couldn't even walk across a room a week before. Another man had had a serious knee injury that mysteriously vanished. Yet a third had a broken kneecap, and another was having upper spinal problems and was wearing a neck brace. The latter two had both been warned by their doctors that it was madness to attempt such a vigorous trek.

However, not only did everyone make the steep climb to reach the cave, but they were glowing by the end. The woman with the neck brace kept repeating Babaji's name the whole way, until she realized that he was inside her taking every step. She felt so deeply blessed and blissful that she was unable to sleep that night.

Is *everything* that happens to us a blessing? Yes! *Everything!!* Even though some things may seem hard, still they are lessons meant for our spiritual evolution.

You might try this: In the morning when you get up, mentally say, "Everything that will happen today will be a blessing from the Divine, meant for my spiritual evolution." Then sometime during the day say, "Everything that is happening is a blessing from the Divine, meant for my spiritual evolution." And, before sleep, with gratitude, say, "Everything that happened today was a blessing from the Divine, meant for my spiritual evolution."

If you do this for one week, with deep belief, it will change your life.

In the flow of divine blessings,

Nayaswami Jyotish

THE DANGERS OF
NARROW MOUNTAIN ROADS

November 12, 2015

THE WHEELS OF OUR BUS were perilously close to the crumbling edge of the road as we drove up into the foothills of the Himalayas. The heavy monsoons earlier in the year had washed away sections of the road, or caused great pits to appear in the middle of it. Both of these obstacles had to be carefully negotiated to avoid tumbling into the valley below or sinking into the gaping holes.

We were part of a group of forty pilgrims driving in two buses from Ranikhet to Drongiri Mountain to spend the day climbing up to Babaji's Cave and meditating there. The two-hour bus ride was not for the faint of heart, as our buses slowly navigated through these obstacles.

It also happened that just as we would hit a smooth patch of road, a large vehicle would often appear around a hairpin curve going in the opposite direction on the one-lane passage. This occurred repeatedly, but thankfully bus drivers in the mountains have experience with such things.

First, there would be a few moments of standoff in which the two drivers would glower at each other. Then, slowly, inch-by-inch, they would maneuver their vehicles in a space of only inches, angling, adjusting, turning, and managing to avoid the precipice on one side or a complete impasse in the middle. With the sides of the buses virtually grazing each other as they passed, each one was finally able to proceed in its own direction.

As we slowly moved up the mountain, the symbolic meaning of the dangers of such roads began to dawn on me. It was like the spiritual path—a razor's edge in which we are always in peril of falling into a pit or off a precipice. Add to this the blocks of impeding karma, and it's a wonder that we can move forward spiritually at all. But there are the experienced guides who can help us maneuver through our bad karma, no matter how impossible it may seem.

In *Autobiography of a Yogi*, Lahiri Mahasaya says:

Attune yourself to the active inner Guidance; the Divine Voice has the answer to every dilemma in life. Though man's ingenuity for getting himself in trouble appears to be endless, the Infinite Succor is no less resourceful.

The spiritual path is filled with far more numerous and dangerous pitfalls than even the mountain roads upon which we drove that day. But we did eventually make it to Babaji's Cave and enjoyed the profound peace found at our journey's end.

May your divine guide ever be with you.

Nayaswami Devi

SIMPLE LIVING

November 19, 2015

As Devi and I took our morning walk through the countryside near our rural Pune Ashram, we were met with a scene that has changed little in the last thousand years. Crops have just been harvested, and the farmers are plowing their small fields with wooden plows pulled by bullocks. They wave as we pass, and we somehow bridge the language barrier by shouting, "Happy Diwali." In India this is the time of *Diwali*, the Festival of Lights, which commemorates light driving out darkness, and is the Indian equivalent of Christmas.

The villagers live a very simple life that has changed only slowly as modern technology makes its inroads. But this simplicity is largely due not to choice, but to circumstances. The simplicity that Paramhansa Yogananda spoke of when he said, "Plain living plus high thinking lead to the greatest happiness" is of an entirely different nature. True simple living is possible when we offer more and more of our attachments to God.

This begins outwardly, perhaps by living with fewer "unnecessary necessities," as Master called them. Rather than feeling deprived, people find that this brings them an increasing sense of freedom. But offering luxuries to God can carry us only so far. We must also begin to offer our time, service, and financial resources — things that we hold precious — and start to test the limits of our non-attachment. But these, too, are still outside of our definition of "self."

Next we must begin to offer up our thoughts, habits, actions, and attitudes: worldly qualities that are the inner enemy forces, the Kauravas, that Krishna urges us to fight in the Bhagavad Gita. Now we enter into another level of simplicity: that of the disciple attuned to the life-changing discipline and love of a guru. At Ananda, members express this by choosing to take vows of simplicity, self-control, and cooperative obedience. But offering even our behaviors and attitudes does not get to the heart of the matter.

Ultimately, what we must offer is the ego itself, our "bundle of self-definitions," as Swami Kriyananda called it. This is best done by purer devotion, deeper meditations, and selfless service. In the Gita Krishna tells Arjuna, "The inner, spiritual fire ceremony of raising awareness is superior, O Scorcher of Foes, to any outward act of self-offering. In this wisdom (alone) is all action (karma) consumed." The daily practice of raising our awareness, through meditation techniques such as Kriya Yoga, offers up the life force itself and brings the genuine simplicity of ego transcendence.

As we continue peeling away the ego, once-bright desires drop away like dead leaves in the fall, and along with them go anxieties, fears, and limitations. In their place we find, not barren branches, but a peace and joy that cannot be found by clinging to possessions and attachments. Worldly wealth can never offer the sense of security that comes through the faith that Divine Mother is providing for our every need.

I see this kind of freedom now in many of my friends and guru-bhais. They seek no thing whatsoever, but only to live more and more purely for God alone. This is true "simple living."

With joy,

Nayaswami Jyotish

WHY OUR PLANS GO AWRY

November 26, 2015

"I REALLY DIDN'T WANT to come on this trip, because I like to be alone and not around a lot of people, but a friend convinced me to go, so here I am," said the slightly embarrassed young man.

It was a strange comment to make, and one that stood out in contrast to what others were saying at the opening circle of our pilgrimage to Babaji's Cave. Most people said things like, "It's so wonderful to be together with this group," or, "I've been looking forward to this trip for many years."

During the pilgrimage itself we didn't get a chance to talk privately with this young man (let's call him "Prem") to see how he was doing, so we never learned what his experience was like until we saw him a few weeks later.

Here is the story he shared: "I had planned to do four things during the pilgrimage. First, although I am a fast walker, I wanted to stay at the back of the line, so that I could think about Babaji and not have to talk to anyone as we climbed up. Next, when I got to the cave I wanted to sit apart from everyone and meditate deeply. After that, I wanted to roam by myself in the hills around the cave, and finally I planned to walk down quickly alone in silence."

With a sweet smile, Prem continued: "None of these things happened. As soon as we began climbing, one of the leaders said, 'Prem, you're a fast walker. Can you go up quickly and carry the harmonium to the place below the cave where we chant and meditate?' I agreed, though inwardly reluctant, thinking at least this would be a help to the others.

"Next, when I sat to meditate, someone sat very close to me who began having leg cramps and shifted around all the time. Instead of a deep meditation, I spent most of the time praying to Babaji to help this guy.

"Then, when I planned to roam in the hills, someone asked me if

106

I could lead the chanting for the pilgrims at the waiting point below the cave. I was reluctant again, but chanted with Babaji in my heart.

"Finally, when I was starting to descend, one of the leaders said, 'Priti is having a lot of trouble with her knees. Could you walk down with her to make sure that she makes it okay?' I could see that she was really struggling, so I agreed."

With joy in his eyes, Prem concluded, "Everything I planned didn't happen, but I'm really glad that I went."

The plans we make for ourselves are often limited by preconceptions of how we think things should be. But God's intentions for us are perfectly designed in the moment for our spiritual growth.

God's plans are always rooted in love: love of the Guru for the disciple, love for those dear to us, love for a stranger in need, or love for those who see themselves as our enemies. If we want to feel His presence, we must cast aside our plans and enter into this flow of love, though we may not know exactly where its current will carry us.

In this season of Thanksgiving, may we be grateful for every opportunity, no matter how inconvenient it may at first seem, to knowingly accept God's plan and offer divine love and kindness to all.

Your friend in God,

Nayaswami Devi

MOTHER, REVEAL THYSELF

December 3, 2015

WHAT AN AMAZING DAY! Six of us were in Pench Tiger Reserve with Satya Prakash, a friend and gurubhai, and a very high official in the Indian Forest Service. He is one of the world's top experts in preserving tigers. India has taken a lead in this area and is helping some eighteen other countries that have tigers still living in the wild. Preserving tigers is really about maintaining ecosystems, because tigers act as an umbrella. When you save a tiger's territory, you also save all the associated plants and animals. Pench is one of the world's best preserves: 400 square kilometers (about 155 square miles), 80% of it banned to people. It is in the Seoni district, made famous by Rudyard Kipling's *Jungle Book*.

The environment has a large diversity of vegetation, which allows a great number of animal species. We had seen many of them: red dogs, jackals, wild boar, thousands of spotted deer as well as sambars, and nilgai. Languor monkeys were everywhere, looking alternately playful and like wise old men. Birds abound and we saw many new ones. The Pench River with its surrounding green belt is like an animal Eden. Unlike anywhere else we have ever visited, this land felt like it belonged to primordial nature and we were only tolerated. We could observe but not intrude. There are only a few roads where people are allowed, under careful restrictions. There are 40–60 tigers here as well as leopards; walking, especially at night, is prohibited for obvious reasons.

We, like all the other visitors, were eager to see a wild tiger. Not everyone is lucky. One man from Canada returned 14 years in a row before he finally saw his tiger. When he did, tears streamed down his face. We drove the roads for many hours, six of us in an open-topped jeep, looking and looking. Finally, it became obvious that we would not see a tiger unless one *chose* to appear.

I began to pray, "Mother, if it pleases you, reveal yourself to us in the form of a tiger." Then, there she was! It was a magnificent encounter: she came walking from our right, less than 30 feet away. These tigers have lived for many generations seeing cars and people, and completely ignore them knowing that they are no threat. The tigress paid no more attention to us than she would have to a boulder. Minding her own business, she first marked her territory with scent and then ambled on to a rare meeting with a male tiger. (I've included a video made on my iPhone.) She was a mother of four nearly grown cubs, and we saw all of them, although the cubs were at some distance.

The experience was deeply spiritual for me. The Divine is omnipresent, but rarely chooses to appear to us. Great yogis such as Babaji appear only when they choose to do so. Otherwise they remain hidden from curious eyes, "hiding behind the sunlight" as Paramhansa Yogananda writes. To see Divine Mother we must yearn for even a glimpse, pray, and be pure of heart. Then She might choose to reveal Herself, in the form of a saint or the spiritual eye, a beggar or a prince, a loving pet or even a tiger. Our job is not to become entranced by Her varied forms, but to see that everything is a manifestation of the Mother of us all.

With great joy,

Nayaswami Jyotish

YOUR GIFTS TO THE WORLD

December 10, 2015

O UR RECENT TIME in India was life changing in many ways. Over time we'll be sharing with you some of our experiences there, but one of the inner transformations that occurred for which we are very grateful is a strong desire for longer, deeper meditations. This grace began during our seclusion in the Himalayas, and has continued upon our return to Ananda Village.

This morning, however, as I began to get ready for meditation, a shade of reluctance entered my mind, and the thought arose, "Do I really have to do this every morning?"

Then I felt a powerful response within: "You are not doing this for yourself alone, but for the good of others. *People of devotion need to send out vibrations of peace and love into the world now.*"

Paramhansa Yogananda said that during the Christmas season the vibrations of the universal Christ consciousness are especially strong on earth, and more accessible to those who are receptive. This is not dependent on whether or not you consider yourself a Christian.

The Christ consciousness (known in India as *Kutastha Chaitanya*, or Krishna Consciousness) is part of the very fabric of creation and of all souls. It can be felt as unconditional love and forgiveness, unity with all people, and an experience of God in everything.

At this time the voices of hatred, violence, divisiveness, and ignorance are screaming so loudly that they seem to drown out the simple song of God's voice in our soul. Now is the time for people of faith in every religion to stand up for good will and righteousness and offer them to the world.

If you are a Christian, fill your consciousness with forgiveness and brotherhood; if you are a Jew, with wisdom and compassion; a Muslim, with the thought that one God blesses and unites us all; a Buddhist, with blessings for all sentient beings; a Hindu, with a sense of God's presence in everything; or a yogi, with a transcendent union with divine love.

These are two gifts that you can offer the world:

1. Pray and meditate until you feel a divine touch of peace or love within you. Then consciously send these vibrations into the world both in prayer and through all your interactions throughout the day.

2. Let the voice of Divine Love in your heart be expressed in whatever ways God makes available to you. It's not enough to sadly shake our heads when hatemongers rant and arouse people's negative emotions. We must actively counter this energy with higher consciousness.

Remember these words of our Guru during this Christmas season:

> I will mentally join in the worship in all mosques, churches, and temples; and perceive the birth of the universal Christ consciousness as peace on the altar of all devotional hearts.

> O Christ, may the birth of Thy love be felt in all hearts this Christmas, and every day.

Joined with you in universal Christ love,

Nayaswami Devi

GIVING THE REAL GIFT

December 17, 2015

WE HAVE A TRADITION at Ananda called World Brotherhood Day. Each year we gather together in a celebration in order to make the first gift of the Christmas season. We suggest that people give one day's income to help spread the light of the Christ consciousness throughout the world. Paramhansa Yogananda explained that the Christ consciousness (in India it is called the Krishna consciousness) is the presence of Spirit at the heart of every atom in creation. When we are aware of this, we feel united with everyone and everything, and, because the Spirit of God is composed of love and joy, we spontaneously want to become a channel for these qualities. The Christ consciousness produces a desire to give to others, which is the deeper reason that people give presents to honor the birth of Christ.

This year at World Brotherhood Day we talked mainly about a remarkable initiative of the Paramhansa Yogananda Charitable Trust. This nonprofit was formed in order to help the poor and disadvantaged. As its first major project we are helping the widows and poor people of Brindaban, the city in India of Krishna's childhood. For centuries widows, rejected by society, have traveled here in the hope that Krishna will somehow take care of them. Societies help them, and many, perhaps 7,000, receive free or very low-cost medical care, blankets, and some food each month. But these donations are not enough, so most are forced to beg in order to stay alive. It is a heartbreaking situation.

The Paramhansa Yogananda Charitable Trust is starting to help in deeper ways. We are helping more than 5,000 with their physical needs, but more importantly, we are giving them love and caring. There is a small staff of very saintly people who go to their homes, talk with them, check on their well-being, and help them with their needs. We have also established three residential houses, filled with that same spirit of love and caring.

These widow-mothers, as they are called, have been rejected by their families and by society, so we are also trying to help them reclaim a life of dignity. To those who are able we offer assistance in finding some means of earning a small income so that they can begin to care for themselves. For instance, Devi and I brought back 150 beautiful hand-sewn japa bags that we will sell, then bring back the proceeds to employ even more.

In essence, we are finding ways to serve as channels of the Christ consciousness, to act toward these widow-mothers as Christ would act, to be his hands and heart. When Yogananda came to America he brought gifts of teachings to ease the spiritual poverty here. In India help is needed also to alleviate physical poverty.

Everything is an expression of God's love, which, after all, is the only real gift we can offer. The money we give at World Brotherhood Day is only a small symbol of our desire to be a channel of the light and love that connect us all.

In the Christ,

Nayaswami Jyotish

THE CHRISTMAS MYSTERY

December 24, 2015

IT IS A GREAT BLESSING to live at Ananda Village, where its members have chosen lives of simplicity, selflessness, and dedication to God. At Christmastime, we often give each other little gifts that remind us of our shared devotion and that inspire us to seek God more deeply. This year two friends gave to everyone copies of a letter that Swami Kriyananda wrote to the community some years ago.

As I read it, tears filled my eyes as memories of so many Christmases with Swamiji flooded my heart. We want to share excerpts from it as his (and our) Christmas gift to you.

Dec 17, 1991

Dear Friends:

Just twenty-six years ago this month I wrote a very special song, one that has remained for many people a favorite among my compositions. I still recall repeatedly wiping away the tears that I might see to write. It was a carol, and I gave it the name, "The Christmas Mystery." The refrain went:

Who'll tell to me this mystery:
How a tiny babe in a manger laid
Could so many hearts to love persuade?
This holy son of Mary.

We human beings have a tendency to look at the world around us superficially. We don't see the deeper realities. When it comes to religion, we view it in terms of its outward labels: Judaism, Hinduism, Buddhism, Islam. Thus, we overlook the essential message, which is one of *inward* reformation. By superficial worship we blind ourselves to the deep truths on which all the truly great religions were founded.

Though we, as human beings, are born into imperfection and limitation, our eternal—and indeed our *only*—mission in life is, through the lessons we learn here on earth, to unite our souls with the infinite Source of all life.

The religious spirit is that aspect of human nature which reaches up in longing for eternal realities. And religion itself is that teaching, and that code of behavior, which inspires and guides mankind toward the fulfillment of this soul aspiration.

Let us then, during this Christmas season, view the birth of Jesus as — yes — a very special event in history, but also as one of the sweetest expressions of universal truth. Let the birth of Divine Love two thousand years ago in that little form inspire us to conceive, and give birth to, divine love within ourselves through the virgin purity of our hearts' devotion to God.

In this way, Christmas can become a holy season not for Christians alone, but for people everywhere on earth, regardless of their outward religious affiliations.

The three wise men, who visited the Christ child with so much respect and adoration, came as representatives of the other great world religions. Let us, like them, open our hearts and souls to Universal Love as it calls out to us from altars of religion everywhere. Thus, may we solve at last that eternal challenge to our human understanding: the Christmas Mystery.

With love always in Him,

Swami Kriyananda

In this spirit, we wish you a blessed Christmas. And you can listen to Swamiji singing this beautiful song, at jyotishanddevi.org/christmas-mystery.

Nayaswami Devi

THE FULL MOON

December 31, 2015

THERE WAS A FULL MOON this year on Christmas Eve, a relatively rare event that last took place 38 years ago. The full moon occurs, of course, when the entire surface reflects the light of the sun back to the earth. As the moon makes its monthly revolution around the earth, it passes through all its various phases, from the new moon when no light is reflected to a half moon and then, finally, the full moon. In astrology, the moon is associated with our emotions. Interestingly, the moon is dark when it is between the earth and the sun, just as our emotions are dark when they get between us and the light.

Paramhansa Yogananda would often say, "The moon gives more light than all the stars." This is an important spiritual image, the esoteric meaning of which is that while the moon (a spiritual master) creates no light of its own, and reflects only the light of the sun (God), it still fills our night with more light than all the stars (egos). Kamala Silva, a great disciple of Paramhansa Yogananda, recognized that he was a perfect reflection of the Divine and entitled her book about him *The Flawless Mirror*.

On Christmas Eve Yulia, a young woman from Moscow staying at The Expanding Light, arose in the middle of the night to walk under the full moon. The night was cold, below freezing, and as she walked she noticed that the ground seemed to be sparkling. The moon was reflecting points of light onto the frozen dew on the dead leaves covering the ground. She took a remarkable video of the thousands of sparkling points of light, which we are delighted (the wrong word, perhaps, even for a punster) to share with you. Here is the link: youtu.be/KTL7rUyFS-Q.

This, too, has a deeper spiritual significance. Beauty and light are everywhere—we need only to look for them. One could hardly think of a better poetic image for despair than "dead leaves in the dark hours of a frozen night." And yet, when seen properly it is filled with light and wonder. Life, too, even in its darkest moments, is filled with God's light. In order to see it, we need simply to still our emotions and open our eyes. And when we see God's light, we can mirror it to others.

Today is New Years Day, 2016. This year, especially, our fragile world needs more sources of light. No darkness can endure where the sun and moon shine. Amidst all of our resolutions for 2016, let us also resolve to be more perfect reflections of God's light and beauty. Resolve this year to become a flawless mirror or, at least, a full moon.

In God's light,

Nayaswami Jyotish

THE SPARK OF A SPIRITUAL REVOLUTION

January 5, 2016

TODAY IS JANUARY 5, 2016—the anniversary of Paramhansa Yogananda's birth. There are numbers that convey some of the historical significance of his life: **123 years** since he was born; **100 years** since he created the Energization Exercises for recharging the body with energy; **70 years** since his spiritual classic, *Autobiography of a Yogi*, was published; and, in 2020, **100 years** since he boarded the ship that brought him to America and began his mission to the West.

But the real story can't be told in numbers. It's the unquantifiable change that he sparked in the lives of millions of people worldwide. Through his decades of lecturing in America, his introduction of Kriya Yoga, and his *Autobiography*, Yoganandaji showed us an expanded vision of reality that we ourselves can attain.

Swami Sri Yukteswar, his guru, said to him on the eve of his departure from India: "All those who come to you with faith, seeking God, will be helped. As you look at them, the spiritual current emanating from your eyes will enter into their brains and change their material habits, making them more God-conscious."

I've been Yoganandaji's disciple now for forty-seven years, and am filled with gratitude for how his presence has transformed me. In 1969, as a typical college student, I read *Autobiography of a Yogi*. Immediately I began meditating, became a vegetarian, then one month later traveled to Ananda Village in California from the Midwest, and have spent the rest of my life seeking God.

I know it would have been impossible for my life to go in this direction without his grace. But my life is not unique: I am one among millions whose consciousness has been changed by this Divine Instrument of God.

During a long meditation on Dec. 23, 2015, a poem came into my mind unlooked for, and kept recurring in my thoughts throughout the day. That evening I decided to call it "From the Higher Self," and I offer it to you, and to my Guru, from whom it came:

> I can't promise that you'll finish,
>> But I know that you'll begin
> To take each step before you
>> With the thought that you will win
> The prize above all others,
>> Your heart's most fervent prayer:
> To cast aside the ego,
>> And to see God everywhere.

This is the ultimate gift of the guru: to awaken our soul's innate longing for God.

With His love,

Nayaswami Devi

WORLD PEACE

January 14, 2016

M ANY YEARS AGO I saw a bumper sticker that said, "Visualize Whirled Peas." I'm afraid that this image, humorous though it was, is truer today than the actuality of world peace. We seem to be whirling around, splintered into frenetic factions. Never, it seems, has there been so much polarization: people divided ever more fanatically along lines of religion, class, and political persuasion. Those of us who are seeking unity with God must also become instruments of unity in the world. How do we do that?

Develop Clarity and Power

With enough concentration and clarity, you can actually begin to materialize your thoughts. To help develop sufficient power in our visualizations, Yogananda gave this affirmation: "Today I will develop the power of visualization and the power of hearing. I will concentrate upon one good thing strongly. I know that if I concentrate for long on a certain image, the life force becomes concentrated in the spiritual eye, reproducing an astral motion picture of that image."

For example, Yogananda said, "When one visualizes a spiritual man and deeply meditates on his mentality and character, one can attract and imitate his spiritual magnetism. For the purpose of exchanging moral, mental, aesthetic, or spiritual magnetism, personal contact is not always necessary."

He also suggested a technique to help develop your memory: "Look steadily at a certain object, or at some scenery, or in a store window, then turn away quickly and see how many of the details you can enumerate. The deeper your impressions, the more details you will be able to remember." Try this with a photo of a saint or image of the Divine.

Concentration and clarity of thought will give power to your prayers for world peace.

Visualization for World Peace

Visualize a globe of blue light at the point between your eyebrows—a light that is both very powerful and innately intelligent. Now let it spread until it illuminates your whole brain, then descends down your neck to fill your whole body. See this light expanding beyond your body, filling the room you are in and permeating your home with warmth and peace. Let the light continue to spread until it fills your town . . . your state . . . your country . . . and finally the whole globe. See everyone and everything bathed with this light.

Now let it touch all areas of shadow or conflict. Feel the glow connecting everyone on a deep, non-verbal level. Let the light take on a vibration of loving friendship, removing all separation. Now, bless the entire world with the Peace and Harmony Prayer.

The Peace and Harmony Prayer

Throughout Ananda, we have started using Yogananda's "Peace and Harmony Prayer" at the end of each meditation or Sunday service. It goes like this:

For one minute (about ten repetitions) repeat: "Lord, fill this world with peace and harmony, peace and harmony."

Then for 15 seconds (three repetitions) repeat: "Lord, fill me with peace and harmony, peace and harmony."

If, collectively, we act as a great lens to focus this peace and harmony, it will illuminate this earth and drive out the shadows. Please join us. Be a channel of God's Light.

In His Light,

Nayaswami Jyotish

WHY POSITIVE THINKING CHANGES OUR LIFE

January 21, 2016

"I'M FEELING SO DISCOURAGED and anxious when I look at everything that's happening in the world today," a friend recently wrote us. It's hard not to respond in this way when we see violence and hatred running rampant across the globe.

But spiritual teachings are not just pleasant sentiments that we dust off and display on a sunny afternoon. They are powerful tools—invincible weapons, in fact—with which to battle the darkness and negativity that we encounter around and within us.

Paramhansa Yogananda repeatedly stressed the importance of positive thinking in dealing with all of life's challenges. He said that you can't drive out darkness by beating at it with a stick. Rather, turn on the light in our consciousness, and the darkness will vanish as though it had never been.

Here are three reasons why positive thinking has the power to transform us:

It Activates Higher Regions of Our Brain

Neurophysiologists are discovering that the prefrontal lobe of the brain, the area located just behind the point between the eyebrows or spiritual eye, is the most advanced part of our brain. When we concentrate there during meditation, we activate that area. This, in turn, enhances our ability to find positive solutions to problems, to develop a sense of well-being, and even to live in a state of unconditioned happiness. It is the seat of what yogis call "super-consciousness."

But there is a wonderful reciprocal process here. When we determine to respond to life with a positive attitude, we also activate the prefrontal lobe. To put it simply, positive thinking enlists the help of our own brain to respond to life with courage, calmness, and even-mindedness.

It Engages the Power of the Universe

Great men and women throughout history have testified that their ability to accomplish their goals was based on the positive, determined conviction that it was possible. Thomas Edison, the inventor of the electric light bulb, tried for years to discover a material that would work for the filament. After nearly ten thousand failed experiments, his friends tried to convince him to give up. With unwavering energy and conviction, he said, "I have not failed, but have only discovered nine thousand ways that don't work."

The universe responds to such determination with the power and energy to press on. And this he did, against all opposition and odds, until he succeeded in creating the light bulb that has changed the world.

It Aligns Us with Divine Joy

Our soul is a little spark of God's consciousness: the Source of all light, love, and joy. Paramhansa Yogananda wrote: "Remember always that positive attitudes uplift the mind, while negative attitudes take the mind slowly downhill into a private gloom. For just as positive, happy attitudes make one receptive to bliss, negative attitudes estrange one from it. In a negative state of mind, one loses sight of the soul's all-powerful ability to transcend every difficulty."

Through positive thinking, we remember that we are God's children, safe always in the harbor of His consciousness.

Your friend in God,

Nayaswami Devi

STORIES AS TEACHERS

January 28, 2016

STORIES ARE GREAT TEACHERS. They involve the listener emotionally, and stick in the mind much better than mere concepts. For example, we all know that that we should think of others and not only ourselves. But the principle comes alive when packaged in a good story. Here is that same teaching delivered by Krishna and Arjuna.

Krishna and Arjuna were walking together one day when they saw a man, dressed in rags, begging by the side of the road. The man explained that he was a poor Brahmin who had fallen upon hard times and that begging was the only way he could feed his family. Arjuna, feeling great compassion, gave the man his entire purse. Krishna, in the meantime, only smiled.

As the Brahmin was going home, a robber, who had been watching, beat him, and stole the purse. The next day Krishna and Arjuna again found the man sitting in the dust with his begging bowl. Upon learning his story, Arjuna, feeling even greater compassion, gave him, off his own finger, a ring with a large ruby. Again, Krishna merely smiled.

This time, as the beggar was crossing the river by ferry to his home, he was filled with great joy and excitement. Unable to contain himself, he held the ring aloft in order to show his fellow travelers his good fortune. As he did so, the boat was rocked by a wave and the ring fell into the river where it was immediately swallowed by a large fish.

On the third day, Arjuna and Krishna again saw the man begging. By now, Arjuna suspected that something more was at play, and asked Krishna what he should do. Krishna smiled again and then gave the man two pice, the least of all the coins of the realm.

As the beggar neared the river, he thought, "What can I do with two pice? Well, at least I can buy the freedom of one fish from the net of the fisherman." Having paid his pittance, he was about to release the fish into the river when he noticed something gleam in its mouth. It was, of course, his lost ruby ring. As he once again held it in his hand, he cried out in a loud voice, "Look what I've found!" The thief, who was in the crowd, assumed that he had been discovered and threw himself at the Brahmin's feet. "Here, take back your purse, but please don't have me thrown in jail." Because of one tiny act of kindness, the beggar had recovered everything.

Arjuna finally understood. And Krishna smiled.

Especially in India children are, or used to be, brought up listening to stories from the great epics, the *Mahabharata* and the *Ramayana*. This is how they learn truth, and values, and wisdom and love. The next time you are about to grab the TV remote control, you might want to reach instead for a good story. As you do so, Krishna will smile.

In joy,

Nayaswami Jyotish

JUST A PLAY OF LIGHT AND SHADOWS

Feb. 4, 2016

"THE MASTER WOULD OCCASIONALLY take some of us to the movies to get away from all the demands on his time," a direct disciple of Paramhansa Yogananda once told us. "Then, in the middle of the most exciting parts, he would tap us on the shoulder, point upward to the beam of light coming from the projection booth, and say, 'It's all just a play of light and shadows.'"

We had a similar experience once with Swami Kriyananda when we went to see the film *Chariots of Fire*, a movie based on the lives of British athletes competing in the 1924 Olympics.

The dramatic climax of the film comes when one of the men is running in his last race of the games. He'd been training hard for several years, and had already lost two of the races in which he was competing. Now had come his last chance to win the gold medal.

As the race begins, the film goes into slow motion; every expression of the runner's face is accentuated; the music reaches a crescendo; and then . . . Swamiji tapped us on the shoulder and cheerfully said, "It's hard to be detached at a moment like this."

We were startled as if out of a dream, realizing how totally absorbed we'd been in the drama. Spiritual teachers and guides keep reminding us to see beyond the experiences of our life to perceive the one reality of God behind it all.

In *Autobiography of a Yogi*, Yoganandaji tells of an unusual experience he had in which he realized this truth.

During World War I, the Master had gone to a see a newsreel of the European battlefields. As he left the movie house, his heart was troubled, and he prayed, "Lord, why dost Thou permit such suffering?"

To his surprise, the answer came in the form of an actual vision of the carnage, which was much worse than what had been depicted in the newsreel. Then a divine voice spoke to him: "Creation is light and shadow both, else no picture is possible. The good and evil of *maya* must ever alternate in supremacy. If joy were ceaseless here in this world, would man ever seek another?"

Yoganandaji goes on to write: "One's values are profoundly changed when he is finally convinced that creation is only a vast motion picture, and that not in it, but beyond it, lies his own reality."

❧ Remember that in the midst of life's tragedies and comedies, we can always lift our eyes to the one beam of divine light from which all of our dramas are unsubstantial projections.

May we all awaken in the One Light of God.

Nayaswami Devi

THE FORMULA FOR SUCCESS

February 11, 2016

WE HAVE JUST FINISHED an uplifting "Inner Renewal Week," which we do annually in February at Ananda Village. In preparing for these classes, a formula for success clarified for me. These are not so much new ideas as they are a clear and simple presentation of them.

You will achieve success in everything you do you when you apply this formula:

Will + Concentration + Intensity + Duration = Success
Let's look at each of these elements more closely.

Will: Paramhansa Yogananda defined "will" as "desire plus energy directed toward a goal." We can fantasize about a goal, or desire a certain outcome, but until we apply energy nothing will happen. Consider the very simple example of closing your fist. You must first want to do so, but until you send energy to the muscles, your fingers won't close. It is will that produces that flow of energy. In fact, Yoganandaji gave us the rule, "The greater the will, the greater the flow of energy."

Concentration: We must next concentrate the flow of energy if we are to produce worthwhile results. A perfect example is a laser, which so concentrates light that it can be beamed all the way to the moon, or used to cut through a thick metal plate.

Intensity: Intensity is similar to concentration, but also different. It involves not just focusing of a flow, but increasing the *power* behind it. A laser powered by a single battery will not work as well as one plugged into a high-voltage power source. An important skill to learn is to relax while still keeping the intensity high. Tension obstructs the flow in much the same way that impurities in a wire will inhibit the flow of electrons through it.

Duration: Finally we must hold the flow, focus, and the intensity on the goal for as long as it takes to accomplish our purpose. Big projects, especially, require a lot of endurance.

This formula can be applied anywhere, in any endeavor: in the classroom, at work, in athletics, for healing yourself or others, or for anything else you might imagine. We observed Swami Kriyananda work miracles in his writing projects through the application of these principles. He wrote the entire 600 pages of *The Essence of the Bhagavad Gita* in only two months. A further secret is that when you apply this formula to a truly worthy goal, you attract powerful universal energies to help you.

Most importantly, this is the formula for success in achieving our spiritual goals. Let's take, for example, the common desire to purify the mind. The aspiration itself will start a flow of energy. A very good way to concentrate and strengthen the flow is to memorize and inwardly repeat Paramhansa Yogananda's prayer demand:

"O Father, Thou art in my mind: I am clear and pure! O Father, Thou art my strength; Thou art my power—I am all Thy strength and power. I am whole!"

If you can focus entirely on these words, your mind will gradually become deeply concentrated. Then, intensify the flow with faith and devotion. Finally, you must hold your focus for a sufficient period of time for the thoughts to permeate your subconscious and superconscious minds.

When we are able truly to follow this formula, miracles can and will happen—I have seen it work many times in my own life. Try it for yourself!

In God's flow,

Nayaswami Jyotish

WHEN GOD CALLS

February 18, 2016

THERE IS A BEAUTIFUL STORY about a devotee (let's call him "Ramdas") whose heart was pure, guileless, and filled with devotion for God. Every morning at the end of his meditation, he would pray, "Lord, whenever You call me to forsake this world, at that moment I will come."

Though God never called, Ramdas still offered this heartfelt prayer daily. Time passed, and he and his wife became filled with great joy, awaiting the birth of their first child. But such is the nature of *maya's* alternating waves of joy and sorrow that his happiness turned to grief when his wife died in childbirth.

As he took the helpless baby in his arms, Ramdas was filled with parental love and the desire to protect this tiny, motherless child. Just at that moment, God broke His silence and called to him: "Ramdas, now is the time for you to leave all and come to Me."

With eyes filled with tears, Ramdas replied, "Lord, You know that You are my heart's first love, and I will come, but I also have a human heart. Please reassure me that this child will be cared for."

In response, God said to him, "Place the infant in a basket, and leave it along the road outside the village. Then wait behind a tree, and see what happens."

Ramdas did as God instructed him, and after a while he heard the sound of many horses approaching. It was the queen of the realm and her entourage en route to a nearby city. At the sound of the horses, the infant awoke from his slumber and began to cry.

Hearing the wailing, the queen stopped the entourage and instructed one of her attendants to bring the baby to her. Ramdas watched in amazement as the queen took his child in her arms, and said, "I will raise this poor, abandoned baby as my own."

His heart reassured, Ramdas quietly walked away into the forest to dedicate the rest of his life to God alone.

This story has always touched me for two reasons. First, it's a beautiful demonstration of God's understanding and acceptance of our human needs. Second, Ramdas's freedom to come when God called gives us all reason to ask ourselves, "What is holding *me* back?"

A friend of ours recently shared a concept that had greatly helped her. She'd become aware of her many "unacknowledged resistances": all the little defenses, self-justifications, and attachments that we allow to remain in our heart. To find the freedom to come to God when He calls, we need to acknowledge and weed out all the "resistances" of ego.

Yoganandaji said, "When will you find God? When all your desires for other things are finished. When you realize that the only thing worth having is Him. When every thought, every feeling is drenched with the love of God."

With joy in the journey,

Nayaswami Devi

THE MONKEYS OF BRINDABAN

February 25, 2016

DURING OUR FIRST VISIT to Brindaban, we were told not to wear sunglasses. When we asked why, our guide explained that the monkeys might steal them.

Recently we heard about this phenomenon in much greater detail from a friend who lives in that holy city. I'm not sure that I should share the sordid and disturbing details with such refined and genteel readers, but sometimes the raw truth needs to come out. The monkeys are organized into criminal rings. It works this way:

A monkey will snatch your glasses from your face and move to a tree or wall just out of reach. There he will wait for you to ransom your glasses. Apparently, in different districts the ransom demanded varies. In one area it might be a banana, in another a sweet drink, and in yet another an exotic fruit. If the ransom is paid, the hostage glasses are released.

If the hapless victim tries to hold out, the level of threat is raised. First the monkey will start to chew on the frame and then, if more incentive is needed, he will threaten to break the frames. Nor is this the end of the matter. Sometimes a group of five or six monkeys will line up, each demanding a reward before the hostage is freed. So, I will pass on this wise advice: If ever you visit Brindaban, don't wear your glasses.

There is a spiritual lesson in this. One of the obstacles to meditation is the "monkey mind." On the battlefield at Kurukshetra, Arjuna's banner had the image of a monkey. The spiritual explanation is that he had tamed the restless mind. Like the monkeys of Brindaban, the mind is both restless and mischievous. And it is a thief. It steals the peace of deep meditation and chatters away until it is paid its ransom, in this case, for the mind to be pulled away from concentration and into thoughts and desires.

Once one mental-monkey starts chattering, he attracts others from his district (chakra). A thought about money will arouse associated thoughts having to do with wealth, possessions, and security. Those of the second chakra will entice thoughts around relationships and sex. The monkeys from the third chakra are mainly concerned with power, position, and authority. When you find yourself in a mental argument, trying to best someone, it is due to the tribe from the third district. Do these monkey-thoughts demand a reward? Yes! And when we "entertain" them, they receive it: There is actual brain chemistry involved, whereby these kinds of feelings and fantasies stimulate pleasure centers in the brain.

So what is the solution? Again I say, *don't wear sunglasses when you go to Brindaban.* When you enter the abode of Krishna at the spiritual eye, look directly into the light. The monkey thoughts can't bother you when you are with Him in your inner temple. They will soon go back to their own business and leave you alone with the Divine.

In the light,

Nayaswami Jyotish

HOW WILL OUR STORY END?

March 3, 2016

In *THE NEW PATH*, Swami Kriyananda writes: "I once had an interesting dream; indeed, it seemed to me more than a dream. I saw myself in another life, deeply devoted to a particular friend. He took advantage of my love for him, and treated me with an unkindness that fluctuated between condescension and outright contempt. In time, there arose in me a feeling of deep bitterness toward him. As I approached the end of that incarnation, I realized that if I died with this attitude my bitterness would, like a magnet, draw both of us back to similar, but reversed, circumstances.

"'Isn't it possible,' I asked myself, 'to escape these waves of retribution right now? Whatever the lessons my friend needs to learn, surely *I*, at least, can free myself.' Then, from the depths of my heart, I cried, 'I forgive him!' At that moment, with a feeling of ineffable relief, I awoke. In that simple act of forgiveness I felt that I had actually freed myself of some karmic burden."

Jesus Christ told his followers that if they had a grievance with one of their brothers, they must settle it before entering the temple. Explaining the inner meaning of Christ's words, Paramhansa Yogananda said that if we want to enter the temple of deep meditation, we first must rid ourselves of any negative energy we hold towards anyone.

How do we do this?

First, look honestly at any resentment or grudges you may be harboring towards others. It doesn't matter if these feelings are justified by the other person's actions towards us—our part is to identify the negativity we're harboring in our own heart, and cast it out.

Next, pray repeatedly for the person until you feel an inward release from your antipathy. Is this quick and easy? No, but the amount of time it takes is determined by the intensity and sincerity of our efforts.

Christ said to love and do good to those who hate you, and to pray for those who mistreat you. He concluded by saying, "Be ye therefore perfect, even as your Father which is in heaven is perfect." Perfection in this case, Yoganandaji explained, means attunement with God and His unconditional love.

Finally, be constantly vigilant so that no new noxious weeds sprout in your soul's garden and choke out the flowers of noble sentiments. The sooner you recognize any weeds of negativity — before their roots become deeply entrenched—the easier it is to pull them out.

Our Guru said, "Reincarnation is created by the satanic force, which has instilled in people wrong desires and attachments, and has influenced them to leave the kingdom of God to return repeatedly to earth—the land of false hopes and suffering."

If we want to find God and end our story of many incarnations, we must earnestly, energetically, and determinedly oppose those tendencies that make us cling to lower states of consciousness. When the ego realizes that we will never let up in our efforts, it eventually abandons the field of battle, and we stand victorious over the one true enemy: delusion. And that is the end of our story.

Joined with you towards victory,

Nayaswami Devi

FLOWERS

March 10, 2016

WE'VE JUST FINISHED a program in honor of Paramhansa Yogananda's *mahasamadhi*, which occurred on March 7, 1952. There is a powerful current of energy that is released on special holy days, especially the birthday of a great master and the anniversary of his passing. Like a surfer riding a giant wave, we can make rapid progress if we make a sincere spiritual effort at these sacred times.

Ananda's celebration took place at a lovely retreat center, *The School of Ancient Wisdom*, near Bangalore, India. Created only twenty years ago, this center already has powerful vibrations, because it was created from divine inspiration and because only spiritual groups use it. While our group of seventy was here, there was also another, similar-sized group dedicated to Babaji, who come here annually. The environment itself is very beautiful, filled with artwork, trees, and flowers. Beauty, in itself, adds a high vibration, reminding one subconsciously of the astral world.

The original Zen gardens started as pleasure gardens or small paradises. Next, they developed into replications of famous scenes, created to save the emperor from having to make an arduous journey. Finally, they evolved into the more symbolically stylized gardens we see now. No matter what the outward form, whenever a garden is created, a little of the astral world descends to earth.

Swami Kriyananda always created beauty around him—in architecture, expansive views, simple but lovely possessions, and especially flowers. Crystal Hermitage, where he lived, is famous for its annual tulip festival. Each April more than ten thousand tulips delight five or six thousand visitors, some of whom have said that these are the most beautiful gardens they've ever seen. Paramhansa Yogananda wrote, "In the flowers and blossoms, with their fragrance and their colorful quilts of petals, God smiles invitingly, as if to tell us, 'Remember Me.'"

Indian devotees enjoy the shapes and colors of God's blossoms, and make amazing altar decorations as a symbol of their love for Him. Whenever we do a program, flower arrangements line the walkway to the temple or satsang hall. Then comes the altar. Ah, the altar! There is rarely anything quite like it in the West. Every picture is adorned with a garland, as is the altar itself. Marigold garlands spill down onto the floor, onto chairs, and sometimes into the entire room.

We recently held an initiation into Kriya Yoga in Chennai, where flower decorations are beyond spectacular. As a part of the Kriya ceremony, each person offers flowers on the altar. In the West, this is usually a single flower, often a rose, or, at most, a single bouquet. Not so in Chennai. Person after person came to the altar, some with trays full of blossoms. Nor did they simply place them in front of an image and leave, as a Westerner would do. They began to decorate the altar. I began, just for a moment, to grow a little impatient with the time this was taking. "Couldn't they be a *little* more efficient?" I wondered. And then I caught myself, and laughed at my folly. Which does God treasure more: efficiency or devotion? As I relaxed, I began first to enjoy, and then to marvel at the love being expressed.

Yes, I thought, flowers are a symbol of God's love for us. And of ours for Him.

In the love of flowers,

Nayaswami Jyotish

THE INVISIBLE CORD

March 17, 2016

THIS EVENING WE'LL BEGIN our journey back from India to the United States after an intense five weeks of travel and sharing with devotees here. Every spiritual seeker needs to come to India at least once in their lifetime, for it's here that enlightened sages perceived the soul's path back to union with God. This awareness lies beneath the surface of every aspect of life.

India is a land of dramatic contrasts: widespread illiteracy and poverty, side by side with rich culture and learning as evidenced by the great poets, scholars, and scientists; excessive materialism and opulence, as well as wandering ascetics and hermits in mountain caves; the squalor in the cities and sanctity in the Himalayas; the mind-boggling diversity of language and culture, as well as the simplicity of God behind it all.

I wish I could mentally transfer to you some of the images of India that will remain vibrant in my heart and mind: the elegant courtship dance of two king cobras as they intertwined with each other at the edge of a field; the peace and depth in the eyes of the new baby born into the Ghosh family at 4 Garpar Road; the sweetness and gratitude in the face of an elderly woman sitting next to me on a plane, when I helped her buckle and later unbuckle her baffling seat belt.

But most of all, I treasure the moments when all separation between individuals has dissolved in shared love and service to our Guru. With gratitude to God for these experiences, I see the melting softness in the eyes of devotees whether in Delhi, Gurgaon, Chennai, Bangalore, Pune, or Mumbai. It is to all of you whose lives have touched ours that we humbly bow and offer our deep appreciation and prayers that God reveal Himself to you.

In the words of our great Master, Paramhansa Yogananda: "There is an invisible cord which binds East and West and all strangers.

Let the Eternal Song echo through your mortal flute, and it will become immortal."

May the Song of God forever echo through all of our hearts, until no other sounds remain.

In God and Guru,

Nayaswami Devi

FULL BLAST

March 24, 2016

ANANDA STARTED AS A retreat rather than a community. It was 1969, and the first few residents had moved to what we now call the "Meditation Retreat." Among them were Swami Kriyananda and I. And Sisi.

Few people know about Sisi. At that time, spring of 1969, she was probably three years old. Today we might call her hyperactive, but fifty years ago she was just thought of as a bundle of energy. She was one of the main reasons we acted so quickly to buy land for the community that was far enough away so as not to disturb the quiet, calm vibration needed for a retreat. Sisi made it quite clear that children and silence do not fit well together. If we were going to build Paramhansa Yogananda's vision of a model "world brotherhood colony," we needed a place where we didn't have to repress the natural buoyancy of youngsters. So within a few months we found, purchased, and moved most of the residents, including all of the families, to the nearby property that is now known as Ananda Village.

At the Village I lived that first year in a tepee, and the next in a tiny travel trailer. In the summer of the third year, 1972, I started building a small geodesic dome that was to be home for several years until a forest fire devoured it. For those of you who have heard the story, this was the dome that leaked so badly.

I had already started living in the dome, even though it was only half finished. The floor of the structure was about three feet off the ground, and I had not yet had time to put in steps. One morning early, I heard something scratching and scrabbling at the entrance. Then I heard a small voice: Sisi had come to visit me, obviously unconcerned about the early hour. But she was having trouble negotiating that jump up to the entrance, for her, around chest high. Then I heard her utter a phrase that has remained with me to this day.

"Hmm," she said, "this is kind of hard. I better use my full blast." And up she sprang.

How do you call forth your "full blast"? Well, enthusiasm is one way. Paramhansa Yogananda said, "The greater the will, the greater the flow of energy." Not thinking something is impossible is important too. We block our God-given power by negative thinking. Sisi didn't block her energy flow. She just wanted to visit her friend and have some fun, and nothing like a missing set of steps was going to get in her way.

Interestingly, Sisi herself gives us the way to high energy. In the Latin languages—Spanish and Italian, for instance—"*si*" means "yes," and Sisi exemplified the spirit of "Yes, Yes!"

So the next time you find something kind of hard, just remember Sisi. Be enthusiastic, have fun, say yes, and call forth your full blast.

In joyful enthusiasm,

Nayaswami Jyotish

HOW TO FEEL THAT GOD IS THE DOER

March 31, 2016

A FRIEND SHARED with me a delightful remark she'd heard recently. She was reading the Bhagavad Gita when another devotee walked by and commented, "That's a really good book. It's a mystery, you know, but I'll tell you how it ends: God did it!"

In talking with others, we're often asked the question, "I hear that we should feel God is the Doer, but how can I actually do that?" This is a subtle concept to grasp, for it seems as if we are the ones who need to make the decisions, and put out the energy to accomplish our goals.

Interestingly, however, men and women of outstanding accomplishments often have a sense that a greater power is working through them. Swami Kriyananda is a good example. The sheer amount of his productivity—books written, music composed, lectures given, communities founded—hardly seems humanly possible.

Yet everything he did was produced in such a flow of energy and grace that he really had no sense of personal achievement. The secret of his creativity was an intense self-offering of his life and abilities to his guru, inner non-attachment, and a humble appreciation for what God had done through him.

Once we were showing a visitor, Swami Shankarananda from Rishikesh, around Ananda Village, and he commented, "At first I couldn't see how Swami Kriyananda was able to accomplish all this. Then I realized he didn't—God did it!"

How do we transfer the sense of "I am doing this" to "God is doing this through me"? Here are two points that may help you.

1. To feel God acting through you, be willing to give more of yourself than you have before. Jyotish and I recently returned from an intensive five weeks of travel, sharing Master's teachings throughout India. It often happened that we had big public programs with little time to prepare or rest beforehand.

All we could do was meditate and inwardly pray that God give us something meaningful and inspiring to share with those attending. Invariably, the inspiration and thoughts came in our moment of need, and we became aware that God was giving us what needed to be said.

2. Try to offer all of your thoughts and actions up to God. The more we can surrender self-will to God's will, the more we will feel His grace and power flowing through us.

While in India, we had a weekend program for Master's Mahasamadhi at a beautiful retreat center outside of Bangalore called "The School of Ancient Wisdom." The grounds were filled with lovely gardens and inspiring quotations posted throughout. One particularly caught my eye:

Speak each word, perform each action, face each situation before an inner altar where you kneel in uttermost adoration and self-surrender, under the sign and seal of your highest Self.

The more we offer our lives wholeheartedly, the more we will feel, as Master put it, that God is "the sole activating power."

In divine friendship,

Nayaswami Devi

SELF-DEFINITION

April 7, 2016

THE GOAL OF the spiritual path is to shift one's self-definition from the ego to the soul. The soul is our true nature, and is aware of its unity with God. But our soul nature is usually hidden from us by the ego.

Paramhansa Yogananda defined ego as the soul identifying itself with a particular lifetime, body, and personality. When the body dies, the ego remains, carrying with it long-term memories, attitudes, habits, and tendencies from the past as it draws us to reincarnate lifetime after lifetime.

Meditation and other spiritual practices help us overcome this egoic hypnosis. But before we are ready to leave it behind, the ego needs much refining. The question, then, is how do we do that?

Swami Kriyananda gave a marvelous definition of the ego as "a bundle of self-definitions." Through many lifetimes the ego's tendencies evolve: from dull and brutish, to clever but self-interested, to altruistic and self-sacrificing, and, finally, to saintly. Only then are we ready to drop the ego altogether and realize that we are eternal beings of light. A vital first step is to let go of negative self-definitions.

The words we use are extremely important. Language is how we articulate our perceptions, but in turn it affects those very perceptions. The words you use to describe someone become the way you view him. The words you use to describe yourself become your self-image. One of the easiest and most powerful ways to refine your bundle of self-definitions is simply to make sure to use positive not negative words. Put simply, *Change your words, and you will change your self.*

When I was about six years old I caught a fish and decided that this accomplishment needed to be immortalized in art. So I drew a picture of myself holding a fishing pole with a huge fish dangling at the end of the line. It needed a caption, of course, so I started writing

"THE GREAT FIS. . . ." But, at that point I realized that I was running out of space on the paper, so I finished the rest, "herman," with small letters. My family, never ones to lose an opportunity for good-natured teasing, began calling me "The Great F. I. Sherman."

Although humorous, the story has a deeper side. I have generally tended to have a positive acceptance of my accomplishments. This leads to having positive expectations and, therefore, courage when undertaking something new or challenging. This quality has allowed me to do many things I might not have tried had I labeled that drawing something negating like "The little boy who finally got lucky, for once." (Besides, that wouldn't have fit on the paper either.)

Train your mind to use positive words. It is not that hard. If the habit of negativity is deep, it may take some time and effort. But, if you are watchful, you can catch yourself and substitute positive terminology for negative. Cease to see yourself as "a failure," and instead become "determined to succeed." See all others, too, through a positive lens. Our words, you see, are self-fulfilling.

Swami Kriyananda once told us, after we had received a critical letter from someone, "You are doing the best you can for who you are." This has long been our fallback position: If we don't feel we have succeeded, we don't say we "can't do it," but rather, "We're doing the best we can for who we are. We'll do it better the next time."

Little steps lead to great accomplishments. Positive egoic definitions lead finally to the only *true* self-definition: "I am one with God."

In joy,

Nayaswami Jyotish

CAN WE CHANGE OUR FUTURE?

April 14, 2016

THERE IS A STORY about a rich man who consulted a psychic to find out who he'd be in his next life. Planning to make out his will, he wanted to know about his future incarnation so that he could leave all his wealth to himself.

Well, obviously this isn't a serious way to affect our future. But both the ancient science of yoga and the cutting-edge science of epigenetics give us understandings and tools for making actual, positive changes in what lies ahead.

More than fifty years ago Paramhansa Yogananda stated that the practice of meditation, and of Kriya Yoga in particular, actually changes the molecular structure of the brain. Modern neuroscience is now validating Yogananda's claim: They're finding that lifestyle changes such as meditation, positive thinking, good diet, and exercise do, in fact, change the brain's structure.

These activities allow us to bring more energy to the brain's prefrontal lobe, which is the center of joy, well-being, and solution orientation. By the same token, less energy is directed to the more primitive parts of the brain that relate to anxiety, depression, fear, and anger. Over time, the way we look at ourselves, others, and the world around us changes dramatically for the better.

But it goes further than this. The latest genetic research is finding that activities such as meditation and positive thinking can even affect our DNA. There are a raft of genes that are changeable in on/off positions. Genetically influenced conditions such as alcoholism, diabetes, and depression can be reset to an off position in our DNA according to our lifestyle, freeing us from their controlling effect.

Not only can you reset what you've inherited in your gene pool to improve your own future, but *you can also pass on to your children the "off" settings of any deleterious genes you have switched off.*

So meditation and a positive mental outlook have a tremendous influence on our future. Yoganandaji said that even if you've been chronically ill throughout an entire lifetime, if at the moment of death you strongly affirm, "I am WELL," you will be reborn in a healthy body.

Swami Kriyananda was plagued with many physical ailments in the last years of his life, but inwardly he never identified with them. Once when he visited a new doctor who was reviewing his voluminous medical reports, the doctor asked him, "How is your health?"

"Excellent!" Swamiji replied. This was how he saw it, and why he was able to keep joyously serving God up to his last day.

"Everything in future will improve if you are making the right spiritual effort now." This oft-made statement by Sri Yukteswar, Yoganandaji's guru, was no mere sweet sentiment. It is a literal truth that shows us the way to glowing happiness, health, and fulfillment: today, tomorrow, and into the uncircumscribed future.

With joy in what lies ahead,

Nayaswami Devi

FIVE ESSENTIAL STEPS TO HAPPINESS

April 21, 2016

PARAMHANSA YOGANANDA SAID, "I once met a very successful and wealthy man, who said to me, 'I'm disgustingly healthy, and disgustingly wealthy.' 'However,' I replied, 'you are not "disgustingly happy," are you?' He admitted he was not. Soon afterward, he became a student of this path."

Happiness is something that everyone searches for but very few are able to find. Here are five key steps that lead to permanent happiness:

1. We must want to be happy.

2. We need to accept guidance to achieve this.

3. We need to apply self-discipline in order to follow the guidance.

4. We need to shift the focus to making inner, not outer, changes.

5. We need truly to accept that both happiness and unhappiness are choices we make.

Let's look more closely at these five steps.

Doesn't everyone want to be happy? Yes, and no. On a deep level, of course, everyone wants happiness. Paramhansa Yogananda said, in fact, that this desire is the fundamental motivation of every living thing. But on a conscious level, very few people seek happiness. Rather, they seek those things that they think will make them happy: money, possessions, relationships, power, fame, etc. The problem with this way of thinking is that nothing outside ourself can ever make us happy. Only we have that power. Why not, then, seek happiness itself, rather than the will-o'-the-wisps that society dangles before us? Happiness lies within.

We need to look for happiness in the right way. At first, many of the ingredients seem counterintuitive, or even counterproductive: non-attachment; serving others; letting go of instinctive patterns such as judgmental reactions, anger, jealousy, and the like. To find happiness requires, in fact, that we transcend the very self that is doing the seeking. We need a guide who is more advanced to lead us along the path.

The need for self-discipline is obvious, but actually to train our will is not easy. Paramhansa Yogananda said, "True freedom is the ability to do what is good and right." Swami Kriyananda's mother once described a self-indulgent relative as having a "whim of steel."

The need to change ourself, again, should be obvious, but most people put much more energy into trying to change others or change their environment than into making inner changes. You will begin to improve only after you accept that the improvement you seek starts within. And that there, too, is where it ends. You can exert at most a gentle influence on others. Remember, they have the God-given right to their own free will. Never make your own happiness dependent upon the behavior of others.

There is a joy appropriate to every situation, even those we think of as unpleasant or disastrous. If you can once really grasp that happiness is a choice, you will have learned one of the most important lessons of all existence.

Ultimately, true happiness is a spiritual quest, and comes from the expansion of consciousness. We must expand heart and mind until we break the chains of ego. These shackles keep us bound, and doom us to the vacillating waves of delusion that keep true happiness forever beyond our reach.

In divine happiness,
Nayaswami Jyotish

Dead yesterday
and unborn tomorrow
what matter them
if Today be sweet
Rubaiyat

IF YOU WANT HIS ANSWER

April 28, 2016

THE ENERGY IN SWAMI Kriyananda's Moksha Mandir, where his physical body now resides, was vibrant with the tangible presence of his love and joy. It was April 21, 2016, the third anniversary of Swamiji's passing, and residents of Ananda Village were honoring him with our annual observance of a six-hour meditation.

A few days before this, I'd had a beautiful dream about Swamiji. In the dream, I was unaware that he had left his body, and was sad because I hadn't seen him for a long time. Feeling a strong desire to be in his presence, I went to his home and found him sitting quietly on the grass.

From his demeanor, I realized he didn't want to engage in conversation, though he did glance up to acknowledge my presence. Speaking quietly to himself, but loud enough for me to hear, Swamiji was reflecting on the long-term effects of many of the things he'd initiated during his lifetime. As he spoke, I began to understand that he wasn't present in the same time/space dimension that I was, but was looking at things from a vantage point in the future.

Swamiji was saying thoughtfully, "Ananda Yoga really changed the direction that hatha yoga was taking in the West from being merely physical exercises to becoming a true spiritual practice. The books that I wrote, too, finally found a wide, appreciative audience and deepened people's understanding of Master and his teachings. And spiritual communities spread on a global scale, creating a new way of life in which people found great happiness."

The dream ended there, but filled me with hope and joy. Why? Because over the years we'd witnessed the tremendous effort that Swamiji put out to launch these revolutionary undertakings, and knew that the immediate results were often less than had been hoped for. Now it was thrilling to hear that over time his efforts really did bear great fruit.

But I believe this dream has another message for all of us. As devotees, it's often easy to become discouraged when we don't get the spiritual results we want. It sometimes seems that no matter how hard we try to meditate, to feel God's presence, or to receive His guidance, our experience never quite matches our expectations.

But remember that through our spiritual practices, we are reshaping our karma and setting into motion new energy patterns that may take a long time to show results. God would not have sent great teachers to guide us, if their teachings were without value. We are sowing seeds for the future, so let us forge ahead with hope.

In Paramhansa Yogananda's beautiful poem, "If You Want His Answer," he has written:

Whether He answers or not
You must keep entreating Him.
Even if He makes no reply
In the way you expect,
Ever know He will respond
In some subtle way.
In the darkness of your deepest prayers,
Know He is playing hide-and-seek
With you.
And in the midst of the dance of life, disease, and death,
If you keep calling Him,
Undepressed by His seeming silence,
You will receive His answer.

With divine friendship,

Nayaswami Devi

TECHNOLOGICAL YOGIS

May 5, 2016

YEARS AGO I READ a short story about an American mountain climber. While gathering supplies in a market in India, he comes across a yogi with matted hair and a long beard, wearing nothing but a simple dhoti. The yogi politely asks the American what he is doing in India. The mountain climber curtly tells this "oddity" to mind his own business. After a rude and arrogant exchange, the American proudly says he is going to climb Mount Everest. The story goes on to describe the long, tedious days of trekking with a caravan of porters to arrive at the mountain and finally to carry supplies to base camp. Then comes the difficult and dangerous ascent to the top, pushing the very boundaries of human will and endurance. What a shock, upon arriving at the peak, to discover this same yogi calmly sitting there in lotus posture. The American stammers, "How did you get here?" The yogi replies, "The question is, 'How did you get here?' Surely you didn't walk, did you?"

Miracles and miraculous powers have long been a central theme when we read books by or about yogis and great saints. People are drawn to these stories like moths to the light, knowing, on some deep intuitive level, that they show the potential that lies within us, too. But because our consciousness is not yet advanced enough to actually manifest these powers, we try to emulate them by physical and scientific means.

Three days ago we had a satsang with the Ananda group in Chennai. As we usually do, we prayed and chanted together, had a short meditation, and then a discourse. This was followed by questions and answers. What was unusual was that, although Devi and I were sitting in a room in California, through Skype we could all see and hear one another nearly as well as if we were actually sitting together in Chennai. I jokingly said that it was like being able to bilocate. Some day, with virtual reality, the illusion will be nearly complete.

There are several trends in technology that give us nearly miraculous powers. Already now, in early Dwapara Yuga (what we might call "the electromagnetic age"), we are seeing nearly instant global communication. When your cell phone rings, you don't know if someone is calling from the next room or from the other side of the world. Soon we will no longer carry electronic devices, but wear them, like clothing or skin. Sri Yukteswar predicted that in this age we would overcome the delusion of space.

Another often mentioned power is the ability to levitate. For those who can't yet achieve this through their own spiritual advancement, there is the hoverboard. Last week a Frenchman rose fifty meters into the air and traveled more than two kilometers over the water, standing on such a device.

Then there is the spiritual state of non-attachment. Through technology we are headed in the direction, at least, of non-ownership. A young person today is likely never to own a car, for example. With the coming of driverless cars plus services like Lyft and Uber, it will become pointless to own an expensive hunk of metal that may sit idle most of the time. Airbnb and other similar new companies are making it possible for people to share underused rooms, assets, and other resources.

I could go on with many more examples of how technology is giving us abilities that would have seemed miraculous only a few decades ago. But, lest we get too excited, these powers exist only in the dream world of the physical plane. Technology, no matter how interesting, can only mimic the powers of the saints. Our job, as true yogis, is to awaken from this dream into the realization of our own infinite potential.

In joy,

Nayaswami Jyotish

WEEDING AND PRUNING

May 12, 2016

"LET'S CLEAN UP these beds," our enthusiastic team leader said as we surveyed the badly neglected herb garden at The Expanding Light Retreat. The lavender, rosemary, and oregano were choked with weeds and dead leaves. Many of the plants looked lifeless or had gone to seed—a sorry sight for people who love gardens.

It was Saturday, May 7, 2016 at Ananda Village. We were celebrating our annual Rajarshi Day: cleaning, repairing, building, painting, planting, weeding, mowing, and tackling many other projects to beautify and uplift our community. Though a steady rain was falling, a group of over one hundred residents had gathered together that morning for our opening circle and prayer.

Started nearly thirty years ago, this annual high-energy event is named for Rajarshi Janakananda, or James Lynn, whose birthday is May 5. He was Paramhansa Yogananda's most advanced disciple and his spiritual successor, and a self-made millionaire by the time he met his guru. Due to his deep concentration and attunement with Yoganandaji, Rajarshi quickly achieved full Self-realization.

Swami Kriyananda said of him, "There were two aspects to his life that are especially important for us. He was a millionaire who became a saint due to the depth of his meditation and devotion. But on the other hand, here was a saint who was able to carry on his worldly affairs.

"There are many of us on the spiritual path who need to be reminded that seeking God is no excuse for not doing a good job at whatever it is we set our minds to do in this world."

So here we were, those of us who were working on the herb bed, bringing our best energy forward as we weeded and pruned the herbs. Weeding is such a perfect spiritual analogy: Weeds are like bad habits. If we pull them out when they're just getting started, they're easy to remove. But once we allow them to remain for a while, their roots get deeply established, and it takes a lot more energy to get rid of them.

Pruning, the trimming back of dead or unwanted growth, also has a message for us. Even though we may be growing spiritually, still it's necessary to look objectively at our patterns of behavior and thought and prune away anything that is diverting our energy from our search for God.

As we served in the herb bed that morning, the rain gradually stopped, and the sun poked out from behind the clouds. In the spirit of Rajarshi, by the time we were finished the garden looked beautiful. We may even have been able to weed and prune some aspects of our own consciousness that were keeping us from God. Certainly, as the sun shone on our backs, we felt His pleasure in seeing His plant children cared for and loved.

With joy,

Nayaswami Devi

SWAMI KRIYANANDA,
A MODEL FOR YOUR LIFE

May 19, 2016

Swami Kriyananda's birthday was May 19—he would have been 90 this year. Often on his birthday a rainbow would appear, sometimes in a nearly clear sky, as if the heavens themselves wanted to celebrate his birth.

Although he had many gifts and talents, he always thought of himself as simply a disciple of his great guru, Paramhansa Yogananda. Swamiji did more than just follow his guru. He modeled his life after him, trying to attune himself completely with the Guru's divine example. I, in turn, have tried to model my life after Swamiji, and, through him, to attune myself more deeply to Yoganandaji.

Swamiji often emphasized the impersonal nature of attunement. He taught us to imitate the divine qualities expressed rather than the personality that was expressing them. Swamiji's form and personality, that we so loved, were only one expression of soul qualities that manifested in many other ways throughout the countless roles that his soul had played. Here are some of these divine qualities as Swamiji expressed them in this life.

Discipleship: This was Swamiji's main self-definition. He sought constantly to manifest the will of his guru. Once he said, "I have long tried to attune my thoughts and actions with Master. But I came to realize that this is not enough. Now I try to attune every feeling also, every breath, with him." His thoughts were often about Master. One time, while we were walking, he stopped and said, "Oh, that's what he meant." He was remembering a moment more than fifty years earlier, and had just understood, from the way Master had raised an eyebrow, that the advice he was apparently giving to another disciple was, in fact, meant for Swamiji. I try to emulate Swamiji by attuning, to the best of my ability, every facet of my life with Master and with him.

Creating New Realities: Most people, resigned to this world as a reality they cannot change, merely grumble about those things they find displeasing. Swamiji was not content with such passivity. Like a king of old, if he saw something that was wrong, he was prepared if necessary to create something entirely new to rectify it. The environment in which most people live is not spiritually helpful, so he created the Ananda communities as a whole new way of life. Since he saw traditional schooling as unbalanced, even unhealthy, he created a whole new educational system, *Education for Life.* Popular music, he felt, was too often downward pulling, so he wrote more than 450 of his own soul-inspired compositions. I could go on, but you get the picture.

Endless Kindness and Support: He was the kindest, most supportive person I've ever met. He loved and cherished not only his friends, but also strangers, who then quickly became his friends. His acceptance of us didn't mean that he ignored our flaws. But he saw past our personalities to our soul qualities, and would go to great lengths to help us grow.

Supremely Non-attached: He was not attached to anything except God and Guru. He didn't care a hoot about money, except as a vehicle to help others. Nor did he identify with his body and its many problems. In serving his guru he had an amazing ability to rise above illness or pain.

There are many other qualities that he modeled for us, too many even to list. If you want to know him better, read his autobiography, *The New Path.* And listen to his music. You will find a divine friend, and a model for your life.

In discipleship,

Nayaswami Jyotish

RUST NEVER SLEEPS

May 26, 2016

THE TWO BROWN BEARS that lumbered past our cabin at Lake Tahoe, California, were larger than I'd ever imagined a bear to be. It was twilight, and a steady rain was falling. Jyotish quietly but emphatically said, "Look," as he pointed out the window: There they were, walking slowly by, not more than fifty feet away. Then, before the bears got out of sight, one of them stopped and shook the rain from his fur like a huge dog. It was thrilling to see them.

We'd come to Tahoe for some relaxation, and were enjoying the stillness and peace of the beautiful lake and woods. The bears were an added treat (although we were grateful that they didn't see us that way).

It's helpful to take breaks from time to time to renew and refresh ourselves. Amidst the demands of daily life, it's too easy to lose inspiration for meditation, and let our practice become mechanical.

"Rust Never Sleeps" is the title of a song that was popular some years ago. It's a great image to convey the potential erosion of our inspiration and joy by the downward pull of demands and problems around us.

Here are four ways that may help you to keep your meditation practice inspired:

Take time out from your daily schedule to focus on your sadhana. Give yourself the freedom to relax and enjoy your meditation without any time constraints. Maybe you'll meditate longer, or maybe shorter, but enjoy the freedom of creating your own space to rest in God.

See the techniques of meditation as helpful tools, not as the final experience you're seeking. An artist uses his paints to capture an image, but the pigments alone don't create a painting. It's the personal consciousness of the artist that brings a painting to life. In the same way, try to see your meditation techniques as a medium to explore your own higher consciousness—it's up to us to give the techniques vitality and life by imbuing them with our own energy.

Feel from the start of your meditation that you're actually a part of a greater reality, that your own higher consciousness is already one with God. Swami Kriyananda expressed this so beautifully: "The secret of meditation is to pray with deep faith—not as an outsider to heaven, but as one whose true, eternal home is heaven." Our "true, eternal home" can be as close as a thought away, if we stop thinking that we are strangers to it, or that it is far away.

Replace the burden of "I should" meditate with the freedom of "I choose" to meditate. Try to bring a sense of relaxation and joy to your sadhana. Remember that, though regular meditation requires discipline, it is you who have chosen this practice, in order to enhance your life. Rust may never sleep, but the search for inner joy is a part of our own nature that calls to us eternally.

Your friend in God,

Nayaswami Devi

CONTROLLING OUR REACTIONS

June 2, 2016

A FEW DAYS AGO my son and I were walking in the beautiful Tahoe National Forest in Northern California. We were enjoying the peace and beauty of this magnificent environment: the trees, the wildflowers, and the little chipmunks scurrying around. We strolled along, talking about this and that with long periods of silence in between. Then the peace was broken by two rowdy, yelling people in a noisy ATV (all-terrain vehicle).

Once they passed, our talk drifted to the sorry state of American politics, where greed, power, and fear seem to have driven out common sense. No, this blog is not going to be about politics, but I am reminded of a bumper sticker I saw many years ago: "If God had wanted us to vote, He would have given us candidates." We didn't remain on this subject for long—the environment was too beautiful to be spoiled by such nonsense.

Our son, although born and raised at Ananda, has not chosen to follow our spiritual path. And yet, a deep sense of good values and dharma seeps from his pores. As our talk returned to more spiritual subjects, he said, "I noticed that I had a really strong negative reaction to those people driving and acting that way. I don't like having such judgmental attitudes. How can I overcome them?" What a great question to build this blog around! Here is some of the discussion that followed.

Our thoughts, I explained to him, follow our feelings, which are centered in the area of the heart, the anahat chakra. Think of the heart area as the sending station for energy or prana. Negative reactions send the energy down the subtle spine, and the thoughts that follow are contractive and self-protective. Positive feelings send energy up, and then the mind supports the rising energy with affirmative reasoning. To control our reactions, we have to start by controlling the reactive process in the spine, and this brings us to the science of yoga. Here are three ways to control the reactive process that I shared with him and now with you.

1. **Breathe Your Way Out.** The recognition of the link between breath, mind, and energy is one of India's great gifts to the world. I recommended to my son that his first line of defense be the breath. "As soon as you realize you are reacting negatively," I told him, "breathe in for a count of ten, hold the breath for ten, and exhale for ten. Do this two or three times and the negative reaction will dissipate like fog under the sun."

2. **Neutralize the Thought.** You can neutralize negativity by introducing a positive thought in the opposite direction. "If," I explained, "as soon as you had the negative thought about the noisy vehicle, you had introduced a positive thought, it would have neutralized the downward flow of energy." I suggested that he think of something good about the people in the vehicle.

3. **Divert Your Mind.** "Think about anything except your judgmental thoughts," I added. Even politics, although the conversation wasn't exactly positive, was at least diverting. It pushed thoughts of that ATV into the background. Once we had regained our equilibrium, it was much easier to get the energy flowing positively again.

The trees and wildflowers worked their magic, and soon we again were enjoying a lovely walk and an even better talk.

In joy,

Nayaswami Jyotish

MOVING BEYOND THE EGO

June 9, 2016

Paramhansa Yogananda described divine vision as being "center everywhere, circumference nowhere." Because God is omnipresent, each of the billions of different perspectives He has created has its own validity. At the same time, no single point of view has a monopoly on truth.

The ego-centered person approaches the world with the thought, "My way is the only right way, and everyone should do what I say." Associating with others of like mind, his life's experiences only confirm him in his point of view.

Devotees, on the other hand, try to live with quite another attitude: "I offer my limited perspective into a greater reality of which I am a small part." Living in this way, their awareness of that greater reality continues to grow.

There is a story of a great sadhu of modern times, Swami Ramdas, who roamed through the forests and villages of India. His hair was long and matted, his clothes mere rags, but he carried within him the bliss of God-awareness.

One day as he entered a village, the young boys spied the sadhu and began to follow him. Absorbed in God, he took little notice of them, even when they began to yell louder and louder to get his attention.

The boys, becoming angry at being ignored, began to fling taunts and then even stones at the sadhu. He continued calmly on his way, despite the fact that some of the stones that hit him drew blood. Returning to the forest, the sadhu was soon surrounded by his disciples, who were horrified to see blood flowing from his wounds. "Master, what has happened?" they cried. "Who did this to you?"

"Oh," he replied blissfully, "the boys in the village had such fun this afternoon. They were laughing, running about, and throwing stones. What a good time they had!"

The sadhu had no center of self-reference from which to react.

How do *we* develop the ability to see the "bigger picture" and break the grip that the ego has on us? In Swami Kriyananda's book, *Sadhu, Beware!* (perhaps our friend the sadhu should have read those words before entering the village!), he gives some suggestions for ego-transcendence:

Never mentally place yourself in competition with others. Competition sets us apart and isolates us; it keeps us from seeing things from a broader perspective. Cooperation, by contrast, joins our energies with others and breaks down narrow fences of self-involvement and rigidity of thought.

When people fail to credit you for something you did and did well, say nothing. Remember that any talent or ability we have comes from God. Give the credit to Him, and find satisfaction in the fact that you were able to serve Him.

Don't let your mind play with the thought of where or how you yourself fit into any picture. Learn to be impersonal in your thinking. Try to focus on "the forest, not your individual tree" in whatever circumstances you find yourself. Don't let self-importance, self-pity, or any self-centered thought rule you.

We are all players in God's dream: equally important and, ultimately, totally unimportant. Our true essence is nothing more than a tiny spark of the infinite consciousness of God. When we can accept this, we begin to know true inner freedom and joy.

Your friend in God,

Nayaswami Devi

ACHIEVING BALANCE
IN AN UNBALANCED WORLD

June 16, 2016

As I travel around the world, one of the questions asked most often is, "How can I bring my life into balance?" People feel pressured and pushed, unable to get centered.

Rebalancing requires effort since we may have to change some long-standing patterns. This is inner work—it is no use looking for help in the world around us. People have their own agendas, and rarely is it to help you attain a state of contentment. One soda manufacturer tested more than 3,000 recipes before it found the exact balance of sugar, flavoring, and caffeine to make people drink more of their product. Put simply, there is a conscious, scientific effort on the part of manufacturers to make their products as addictive as possible.

So, how do we get centered in an unbalanced world? We have to return to our core values. It might help to visualize balancing a ruler on your finger. You've probably done this as a child, continually moving your hand back and forth to keep the ruler upright. Without realizing it, you are trying to align the top and the bottom of the ruler with the earth's center of gravity, or its core. This is a good symbol for what's needed: to align your habits and activities with your own center of gravity, your core values.

We are physical, emotional, intellectual, and spiritual beings, and it would be very helpful to spend a little time meditating on your aspirations in each of these areas. Here are some general goals to start, but you'll need to do your own thinking about personal directions:

Physical: To be healthy, strong, flexible, and energetic. To achieve this, we need to regulate our diet, sleep, and exercise, and to avoid toxins such as alcohol, smoke, and drugs.

Emotional: To be even-minded and cheerful.

Intellectual: To keep our minds sharp, creative, and able to concentrate deeply.

Spiritual: To achieve Self-realization, or union with God. This is the ultimate purpose of all life and the most important goal of all. Is it the center of your world? If you focus your life around your spiritual quest, everything else will begin to fall into place naturally.

Start and end every day with God contact. Devi and I have a picture of our guru, Paramhansa Yogananda, on the wall facing our beds. It is the first thing we see in the morning and the last at night. This helps us stay centered in God. Paramhansa Yogananda said, "It is very difficult to find the right balance between work and meditation. You will achieve a good balance, however, if you work in the thought of God during the day, and meditate on Him deeply at night."

Rebalancing involves clarifying our core values and making them our priorities. It takes resolve. But to paraphrase Krishna in the Bhagavad Gita, "Even a little effort toward achieving balance will free you from dire fears and colossal sufferings."

From my center,

Nayaswami Jyotish

FROM CONCENTRATION
TO ABSORPTION TO . . .

June 23, 2016

SOME YEARS AGO we were completing the work on Swami Kriyananda's dome at Ananda Village, the initial building of what has evolved over time into Crystal Hermitage. Although the interior of the dome still needed work to transform it from a building site into a home, Swamiji was eager to move in.

To speed up the process, he rounded up a group of us after meditation one morning and asked if we would like to help him paint the interior walls. Did we ever! It was always a joy to spend whatever time we could with him.

By the time we all assembled at the dome, it was about ten o'clock in the morning. Swamiji worked alongside us, and we painted steadily and silently until noon. Then he suggested that we take a break for meditation and lunch, and reconvene at two o'clock.

When I returned after the break, I was asked to paint the wooden beams of the large hexagonal picture window which overlooks the Sierra National Forest. Because the wood was rough, it was a difficult task. Standing on a stepladder, I had to concentrate on every inch and apply multiple layers of paint to get an even coverage.

The more I painted, the more I became absorbed in the process, and lost all track of time. As I forgot myself in the task at hand, there grew a sense of joy, and of oneness with a greater reality.

After what seemed like a few hours, Swamiji, looking around and seeing that the painting of the dome was done, said, "Well, everybody, thanks for all your help. It's time to call it a day." I looked at the clock, and it was three o'clock the next morning! Unaware of time's passing, we had happily painted through the night without any fatigue.

Swamiji gave us a great blessing through that experience: He showed us how concentration, when held in a carrier wave of uplifted consciousness, turns into a sense of joyful absorption and expansion of awareness.

In his classic *ashtanga yoga* (eightfold path), Patanjali wrote that the path to enlightenment embraces eight stages. The sixth of these, *dharana*, can be described as concentration, or fixed inner awareness. The seventh is *dhyana*, meaning meditation or, more properly, absorption.

Our mind becomes absorbed in the object of our concentration. If we concentrate on our faults, we strengthen those faults. By concentrating instead on positive qualities, we ourselves become more positive. And by concentrating on the inner light, or upon any divine reality, we gradually take on the qualities of that inner reality.

The eighth and last stage of the eightfold path is *samadhi*, or oneness. Swami Kriyananda has written: "Once the grip of ego has really been broken, and one discovers that he *is* that light, there is nothing to prevent him from expanding his consciousness to infinity."

In whatever you do, whether in the company of others or alone, and especially in meditation, give it your fixed awareness. That will lead you to absorption, and eventually to oneness with all that is. It's not that hard!

With joy in our Guru's teachings,

Nayaswami Devi

MOUNTAINS, OUTER AND INNER

June 30, 2016

WE VISITED ANANDA'S Seattle community last week, where a friend, knowing of my love of mountains, gave me this poem of Hafiz:

> The beauty of the mountain is talked about most from
> a distance,
> Not while one is scaling the summit with life at risk.
> That is the time for silence, one-pointedness, reflec-
> tion, and drawing upon all your skills
> So you might return from the cloud's domain and in-
> spire others to breathe closer to God,
> While still human, the way you did.

We all have our mountains to scale, though they are usually inner crags of our own creation, thrust upward by conscious choice or by the echo of past karma. When faced with a peak that seems too steep, we need to call for help. We need not shout, only whisper. But if we do not call, we will likely end in a fall. We can call in this way:

Ask of God or Guru these two questions:

"What should I do next?" This simple question will save you from many a plummet.

And then, once the course is set, *"How should I proceed? Show me where next to place my feet and hands."*

The first and greatest challenge is simply to remember to ask: God does not mind our failures, only our indifference. The second challenge is to actually follow our inner guidance. A friend once lamented to Swami Kriyananda, "It is so hard to know what to do." His classic reply was, "No it isn't. You already know the answer. Your problem is *doing* what you know to be right."

Determined action is needed. Swami Kriyananda told the story of a fellow monk who had been a famous mountain climber. One time, while making a first ascent in the Alps, this man arrived after a long and difficult climb at a ledge from which point the mountain curved up and out. Able neither to proceed nor to return, and facing near certain death, he decided that it was better to climb than to stay and starve. As he reached the point where he was upside down, he fell back onto the ledge. Again he tried. And again, and again. After numerous failures, he felt a force, as if a giant hand were holding him against the mountain. He was able to get past the overhang, and from there to reach the summit without further difficulty. The descent down the other side of the mountain was easy.

Unlike a mountain, the guru is conscious and eagerly awaits our call, a call that sometimes might not be consciously directed to Him, but issued none the less through courageous action. If we open our heart to Him, He will enter to give us both the guidance we need and the grace to overcome our challenge.

Once we have scaled our mountain, we will have a precious gift to share. To others who are struggling, we can be a guide along the route that leads ever upward. As Hafiz says, we can "return from the cloud's domain and inspire others to breathe closer to God."

In divine friendship,

Nayaswami Jyotish

THE TREASURE BOX

July 7, 2016

"THIS IS ALL I was able to rescue from our house before the fire forced me out," Jyotish said as he handed me a small cardboard container slightly larger than a shoebox. It was the end of a long day on June 28, 1976. The forest fire that had started that morning, and that burnt Ananda Village to the ground, was finally contained.

I knew what was in the box.

Earlier that morning I'd decided to give our house a thorough cleaning: it had been neglected ever since our son had been born eleven days before. Having almost finished with the job, I turned to clean our meditation room, when I realized it was time to leave for a medical appointment for our baby. Seeing how dusty the room had become, however, I was reluctant to leave the many sacred objects there in such a state.

Looking around, I found a small cardboard box; carefully I placed everything from the altar inside it. Among the items precious to us was a silver container with a strand of Yogananda's hair, a rudraksha mala blessed by Anandamayi Ma, two little vases given to us by Swami Kriyananda, and a picture of Master that had been with me since I'd come to Ananda seven years earlier.

I left the box by the entry to the meditation room, which was only a few feet from the front door. Taking our son in my arms, I glanced back at the house, and felt gratified that everything was now in order. "I'll clean the altar after I return," I thought.

That was the last time I ever saw our home. The intense fire that struck Ananda that day burned down all the existing houses and even melted wrought-iron woodstoves. Still, Jyotish, who had been fighting the fire, was able to run inside our home in the few minutes left to him, and grab the box of treasures he spied by the door.

In the weeks and months ahead as we moved from one temporary dwelling to another, that box was our security, our strength, and our reminder that God was always watching over us. Never did we feel despair, discouragement, or even a sense of loss, but only an inward clarity about how to move forward. Over time Ananda Village was rebuilt, and stands today as a manifestation of Paramhansa Yogananda's vision of world brotherhood colonies.

We still have those precious items, carried with us during a lifetime of serving God: They have been with us in many homes in different countries. What a great gift that box was to us! The little items it contained will one day turn to dust, but we will have always with us the imperishable knowledge that God's presence is the only security in our lives.

In *Conversations with Yogananda*, Swami Kriyananda recounts the following story:

"A visitor to Mount Washington Estates," the Master told us, "once inquired of me superciliously, 'What are the assets of this organization?'

"'None!' I promptly replied. 'Only God.'

"Divine Mother once told me, 'Those to whom I give too much, I do not give Myself.'"

May God be the sustaining power in your life.

Nayaswami Devi

LESSON LEARNED, LESSON REVIEWED

July 14, 2016

T HERE WERE ONLY a few occasions when Swami Kriyananda corrected me strongly. At the time, I thought he was "upset" with me, but later I realized that wasn't really true. It was rather that I needed something strong enough to break through any resistance I might have had. Here is a story about one of those times.

It was in the late 1970s. Swami Kriyananda had been invited to lecture in New York City. While there, he wanted also to return a visit to Swami Satchidananda, who had visited Ananda in the very early years of the community's existence. Swamiji and I stayed in the Manhattan apartment of a friend.

One evening I received a phone call from one of our members, a contractor, at Ananda Village. Carpentry was one of the few jobs that paid well, so a number of our family members worked in that trade. The contractor called to say that they were having a very hard time financially, and with a lot of negative emotion complained to me that the "leadership" (meaning primarily Swamiji and me) was not supportive of him or, in general, of those doing business. I probably resonated with his distress, since Devi and I, with a baby, were struggling financially too. At any rate I, in turn, related the conversation to Swami Kriyananda with a good deal of agitation.

He looked at me and said firmly, "I am doing all I can. Others have to take responsibility for their part of this work." He then went into his room and closed the door. He didn't come out for the rest of the evening. By the morning, I had come to my senses and apologized for my behavior of the previous evening. He simply said, "Good. You needed to apologize." After that, the incident was never again mentioned nor was there any hint in his behavior that anything had even happened. For me there were many lessons about how to behave when there is a potential dispute. Here are some:

Be centered: Communication doesn't work if you are in a negative emotional state. When you are calm and centered you can discuss, otherwise you will argue.

Be nonreactive: Swamiji didn't return my negativity. He stated his truth simply, quickly, and without defensiveness.

Be loving: He never withdrew his love and support, during or after the incident.

Be a model: He didn't *tell* me how to behave, he modeled right behavior for me. Action is a better teacher than words.

Be able to distinguish: He saw me as a soul and, while he corrected my behavior, he never told me that *I* was negative.

Be done: Once I accepted the lesson, it was never mentioned again.

Life is a school. I learned a lot at that time, and even more from reviewing it in the dispassionate calm of distance. Be deeply grateful when your lessons are presented clearly and powerfully. Accept your tests, learn your lessons, and move on.

In divine friendship,

Nayaswami Jyotish

BREAKING FREE OF OUR KARMA

July 21, 2016

People frequently ask us, "Why have you followed the spiritual path for your whole life?" There are many answers to that question, but a big one is: "It brings me inner freedom." By this I mean, freedom to change negative patterns that have kept me in their clutches; freedom to respond with calmness and kindness even when others are angry or challenging; and, simply, freedom to enjoy whatever life brings.

We've all had those painful "Aha!" moments when we look in the mirror and realize that *we've* actually been the cause of a lot of the problems in our life. Swami Kriyananda gave some great advice for such times: "When you see a fault within yourself, don't despair, but rejoice. It's been there all along, but now that you've seen it, you can start working to change it."

So what are some spiritual tools that help us to break free of our karmic patterns?

Karma is simply energy generated by past thoughts or actions that we've steered in a certain direction. This understanding gives us a handle on the subconscious patterns that control our behavior, and the ability to direct the flow of energy in a positive direction. With conscious awareness and determination, replace a negative pattern with a positive one.

If, for example, you've been critical of others, attracting in turn criticism back to you, use your will power to offer acceptance and support to everyone. Though the battleship of our karma may be slow in changing its course, in time a new direction will be set, heading us now toward the open seas of freedom.

Use affirmations repeatedly with deep concentration to change chronic patterns of thinking. Find a prayer or affirmation appropriate to a specific karma that you're working on, and let it be your constant companion. For example, if you have a problem with mindless snacking, use these words of Paramhansa Yogananda whenever temptation comes: "Today I will rise above the consciousness of food and know that I live by the pure peace of silence. I will feed my soul constantly with the Divine Manna of Peace."

Be patient: The deeper the karma, the longer the time required to change it. As Master recommends, don't constantly dig up the spiritual seeds you're sowing to see if they're taking root. Let them grow in their own time to become mighty plants.

Bring the problem to God in meditation and prayer. Some years ago I was faced with a test that was causing me a great deal of pain. No matter what I did to free myself from the clutches of this karmic beast, it tenaciously confronted me every day. Finally I went to Swami Kriyananda to ask his advice about how to break free of it.

With wisdom and love, he said, "Everything that you're doing is good, but ultimately it's God's grace that frees us from our karma."

From his words I understood that our sincere efforts and desire to be free draw the grace that brings release. We have to do our little part, and then God steps in and unties the knots of karma that have kept us bound.

And so it happened in my situation. Though it took some years, ultimately the karma was dissolved in an unexpected, beautiful, and deeply satisfying way that I couldn't have envisioned myself.

Through the grace of God and Guru, may we find freedom from all limitations.

Nayaswami Devi

SHARE YOUR LIGHT

July 28, 2016

IN 1974 I WENT on a trip around the world with Swami Kriyananda. Our small group started the journey by flying from San Francisco to Hawaii. While there, we had dinner at the ashram of Subramuniyaswami on the island of Kauai. The meeting between Swami Kriyananda and Subramuniyaswami was a delight to behold. They were like twin souls, both having founded spiritual works and ashrams based on the deep teachings of India.

As we were preparing to leave, Subramuniyaswami said something I have never forgotten: "You have brought your light to this ashram, and we have added our light to yours. Now, as you travel, bring this light with you, wrapping the globe with strings of light."

The image of wrapping the planet with strings of light has remained with me ever since. When we traveled from Kauai to India, we tried to follow this advice. As we met Paramhansa Yogananda's brother and visited his boyhood home, we felt the blessings and shared our own. As we sat at the feet of Anandamayi Ma, I absorbed her grace and have shared it ever since. As we meditated in the great pyramid of Giza, I tried to absorb its high vibrations, and as we continued on to Rome and Assisi, with their long tradition of saints, I did my best to receive their light and to add my own. And now it has become a lifelong habit.

The Divine has ever conferred upon spiritual seekers the responsibility to share the light. This, especially, is what we all must do during this period when there are people and forces that are trying to darken this beautiful world. When there are terrorists or politicians who seek to extinguish every light that does not fit their ego-limited world view, it's a time when those who love the divine light must redouble their efforts to relight those lamps.

How do we spread light? First, we need to find the light within ourselves. Light will appear in your forehead during deep meditation. Gaze into that light and absorb it into your consciousness. Swami Kriyananda told us to relate to others from our spiritual eye to theirs.

Again, in inner stillness, the light of love and kindness will begin to blaze in your heart. Feel it there, let it expand, until you feel it as God's universal love. Then share it. Share it in your meditation by visualizing a loving light spreading around the planet, touching every country and every heart with its tenderness. It is helpful to keep a prayer list to focus your efforts. Devi and I have such a list on our altar and pray daily for people and places around the world.

Finally, take your light with you as you go about your daily tasks. Every day will present you with someone who needs love or encouragement. Every day you will see places where someone has cast a shadow by their hatred or negative judgmental attitudes. Be an agent for God. *the Divine* As the beautiful prayer commonly attributed to St. Francis* goes:

Lord, make me an instrument of Your peace;
Where there is hatred, let me sow love;
Where there is injury: pardon;
Where there is error: truth;
Where there is doubt: faith;
Where there is despair: hope;
Where there is darkness: light;
And where there is sadness: joy.

This is not mere sentiment. It is a call to action. We live in a time when there are people who would purposely sow hatred, doubt, and darkness. We must not be idle while another child is maimed or another million are deported from their homes. It is a time to do our part to wrap this world in strings of light.

In joy,

Nayaswami Jyotish

---

* The prayer in fact was not written by St. Francis. (See, for example, www.nytimes.com/2009/01/23/world/europe/23italy.html.) An interesting tradition within the Roman Catholic Church states that it was written by William I ("the Conqueror") of England. (See, for example, the article by Fr. Albert Haase O.F.M. in the January 1999 issue of St. Anthony Messenger, where he writes, "Scholars have found the earliest version in the breviary of William the Conqueror.")

COURAGE

August 4, 2016

IT WAS A BITTERLY COLD winter, and the men were starving and ragged. Many of them were barefoot, and all of them without hope. The year was 1776, the low point for the Americans in the Revolutionary War against England.

General George Washington was struggling against overwhelming odds to keep his troops from deserting and to rally them to face the power of the British army. A new nation—one based on freedom and equality—was desperately trying to take life; by all outer indications, it was going to be stillborn.

Then Thomas Paine, an aspiring writer who had emigrated to America from England two years earlier, wrote a series of pamphlets called "The American Crisis." The first of them began with these words:

These are the times that try men's souls. The summer soldier and the sunshine patriot will, in this crisis, shrink from the service of their country; but he that stands by it now, deserves the love and thanks of man and woman.

The pamphlet was published on December 23, 1776. Its impact on General Washington and his troops was such that two days later, on Dec. 25, they crossed the freezing Delaware River at night, and soundly defeated the British at the Battle of Trenton. It was the turning point of the war.

Where does such courage come from? The word itself comes from the Latin root "cor," meaning "heart." It is from within our heart that we find the strength to enter a battle against overwhelming odds; to confront a foe stronger than ourselves; to face inner tests that have always defeated us.

How do we find our inner source of courage?

Find what is dear or important to you in life and fight for it; then forget about the results. As Master explains so profoundly in his commentaries on the Bhagavad Gita, life itself is a battlefield. We must take up our sword, do what is before us, and be unattached to the outcome.

Every test in life is a test of our will power. Challenge yourself daily to strengthen your will power: first in little ways, and then in increasingly demanding ones. Eventually you'll reach the point where nothing can stand in your way.

Call constantly on God's power to give you the strength and courage that you need. Here are some words of Yoganandaji to one of his disciples:

> You must never lose courage. . . . Overcome all by constant inward calling on God and utmost devotion in words, thought, action, and obedience to Guru. . . . Your troubles I do not mind. I will never give up my job about you. . . . Have no fear, even when I am gone and no longer visible to your eyes. You will never be alone. . . . I shall ever be with you, and through Divine Mother guard you from all harm, and will constantly whisper to you guidance through your loving self.
>
> So do not be discouraged or tired, but be ever interested in doing for Divine Mother, no matter if war, sickness, and death dance around you. . . . A smooth life is not a victorious life. And I will give you lots of good karma, so you will get through.

Towards divine victory,

Nayaswami Devi

THE THIRD WAVE

August 11, 2016

THE FIRST OF THREE great waves of blessing for mankind began in 1861 in the Himalayas. It was then that the great avatar Babaji initiated his disciple, Lahiri Mahasaya, into the yogic science of Kriya Yoga. As he was about to return to his job and family, Lahiri pleaded to Babaji, "I pray that you permit me to communicate Kriya to all seekers, even though at first they cannot vow themselves to complete inner renunciation. The tormented men and women of the world, pursued by the threefold suffering, need special encouragement. They may never attempt the road to freedom if Kriya initiation be withheld from them."

Thus the blessing of Kriya became available to sincere men and women like you and me. This first wave was, however, confined to India. Among Lahiri's many disciples were Yogananda's parents and his guru, Sri Yukteswar. During his years in India Yogananda was prepared for his divine mission, to bring the science of meditation to the millions of thirsty souls in the West.

The second wave began with Yogananda's coming to America in 1920, where he lectured and wrote tirelessly. In the next 30 years he personally taught more than 100,000 people the ancient science of yoga and Kriya meditation, and planted these practices in the mindscape of America. His mission was to uplift the consciousness of a whole culture, and to knit together East and West. It culminated with the publishing of *Autobiography of a Yogi*, one of the most influential books ever written.

And yet that book is not meant to be just read. It needs to be lived. It is an owner's manual for how to live a happy, successful, and holy life in these modern times. Another, third, wave was needed to *demonstrate* that these teachings are practical in the home, and the workplace, and the schools; that they are effective in health and sickness, in birth and death, and not only in the church. This third

wave started in, of all places, Beverly Hills, California. As Swami
Kriyananda writes in *The New Path*:

> I remember especially how stirred I was by a talk he gave at a
> garden party in Beverly Hills on July 31, 1949. Never had I
> imagined that the power of human speech could be so over-
> whelming; it was the most moving talk I have ever heard.

> "This day," he thundered, punctuating every word, "marks
> the birth of a new era. My spoken words are registered in the
> ether, in the Spirit of God, and they shall move the West. . . .
> Self-Realization has come to unite all religions. . . . We must
> go on—not only those who are here, but thousands of youths
> must go North, South, East, and West to cover the earth with
> little colonies, demonstrating that simplicity of living plus
> high thinking lead to the greatest happiness!"

This third wave is *our* golden opportunity. If we live our lives in
attunement with the Divine within us, and practice a life of meditation and selfless service, it will lead to our own greatest happiness.
But, more than that, this third wave can fulfill Master's promise of a
new and better era for the whole world.

In joy,

Nayaswami Jyotish

GOING BEYOND THE RESTLESS MIND

August 18, 2016

IN *AUTOBIOGRAPHY OF A YOGI,* Paramhansa Yogananda describes the scene in which he had his first experience in this lifetime of cosmic consciousness. It occurred when Swami Sri Yukteswar, his guru, tapped him lightly on the chest over the heart, and the breath was drawn out of him.

Yogananda writes: "An oceanic joy broke upon calm endless shores of my soul. The Spirit of God, I realized, is exhaustless Bliss; His body is countless tissues of light. A swelling glory within me began to envelop towns, continents, the earth, solar and stellar systems, tenuous nebulae, and floating universes."

Swami Kriyananda explained that when Sri Yukteswar tapped Master on the chest, what occurred was the complete interiorization of his *prana*, or life force. When our prana is totally interiorized, we become breathless, and can then enter a state of deep stillness. All restlessness ceases, and we become absorbed in awareness of God's presence.

For most of us who practice meditation, the restless mind is our greatest obstacle. No matter how sincere we are, or how hard we try to overcome intruding thoughts, it seems nearly impossible to achieve calm, focused concentration. Yoganandaji's experience, however, offers us a clue for how to accomplish this.

Unwanted, restless thoughts are only energy patterns in our mind. Like weeds in a garden, we can keep pulling them up, but as long as we continue to water them, they will persist. It doesn't help to blame the garden or feel guilty that we are bad gardeners. The secret is to cut off the "water," the life force, that is feeding them.

When we interiorize our prana through attunement with the guru and the practice of techniques like Kriya Yoga, we begin to transcend the restless mind. Kriya Yoga and other similar techniques enable us to direct our prana inward and upward to higher centers of awareness.

For most of us, this doesn't occur right away, but over time we can "reverse the searchlights of the senses," as Yoganandaji described them. Eventually we become accustomed to being in a state of focused, inner awareness, and the molecular structure of our brain even changes to support our efforts.

But as long as our prana is moving predominantly outward, we are plagued not only with restlessness, but with all the desires and longings for outer fulfillment that it awakens. We live in the perpetual thought: "I know I would be happy if only. . . ." You fill in the blank.

In Swami Kriyananda's beautiful song, "God's Call Within," he writes:

> Friend, how long will you wander?
> Friend, as long as you seek your home
> In a land where all are strangers,
> Love locks her door. . . .
> Turn, turn, turn within:
> In silence of soul, in cave of love
> Find My abode.

In divine friendship,
Nayaswami Devi

THE REIGN OF KING DWAPARIAN

August 25, 2016

Aᴄᴄᴏʀᴅɪɴɢ ᴛᴏ ᴛʜᴇ ancient teachings of India, there is a great repeating historical cycle of four ages, called the yugas, which lasts 24,000 years. For 12,000 years the consciousness of man rises to its height, and then begins a 12,000-year descent into darkness. Our current age, Dwapara, is in the ascending half of this cycle. It started in 1700 and will last for 2,400 years. The scale of the yugas is so large that it is hard to visualize, but if we divide by 100 it will help us see the major trends. For fun, then, let's think of a king named Dwaparian ruling this beautiful, blue island called Earth. His reign will last 24 years. With so many people feeling hopeless about current events, it is important to realize that we are only a little over three years into his rulership.

Dwaparian is remarkably energetic, creative, and inventive. He has a keen interest in science, especially in anything having to do with energy. He travels a great deal, increasingly thinks of the whole world as his own, and is very interested in anything that can reduce the sense of space.

Unfortunately, he is not particularly high-minded, and tends to be self-focused, self-indulgent, and somewhat greedy. He puts his own interests first, and doesn't share well, which causes lots of squabbles and fights. Here are some of the major trends of his kingship:

Energy: When he came to his kingship, the bodies of men and animals still provided most of the power. Dwaparian had a strong desire to replace physical labor with increasingly sophisticated machines, but he needed energy. First came steam power, then the discovery of oil and gasoline, and soon thereafter electricity. At the beginning of his third year, the atomic age was born.

A shrinking world: Along with the discovery of new energy sources, new forms of transportation and communication emerged, which increasingly shrank the world. Steam locomotives, and then the internal combustion engine, allowed rapid movement of goods and people. Then came airplanes, jets, and rockets, which both shrank the planet and allowed mankind to expand into space. Soon to come will be driverless cars, widely used robots, and artificial intelligence, eventually eliminating the need for physical labor and repetitive work. Ideally this should free men and women for higher pursuits.

Even more than transportation, communication devices have begun to shrink the planet. It started with the telegraph—the eruption of Krakatoa in Indonesia in 1883 was telegraphed immediately and followed around the world. The telephone soon followed, then radio, television, the internet, and smartphones, connecting people instantaneously with one another. Now this trend is producing extreme miniaturization in everything from electronics to medicine.

The downside of Dwaparian: His realm is plagued by greed, insensitivity, and excessive restlessness. Greed brings economic imbalance, depressions, and class conflict. Insensitivity allows the exploitation of the environment, causing climate imbalance. And Dwaparian's realm is becoming overly complicated and stressful. These trends will be disastrous if allowed to continue.

Man's greatest hope: Soon after Dwaparian began his reign, God sent great avatars to help guide and uplift the world. All of man's inventions and power mean little, and in fact pose a threat, unless the general level of consciousness can be raised. It is the mission of Paramhansa Yogananda, in particular, to serve as a way-shower for this new age. And it is the mission of Ananda to share that message. Only when Dwaparian learns to live in attunement with the Divine can he create a happy and wise kingdom.

In peace,

Nayaswami Jyotish

WHAT AWAITS US

September 1, 2016

IN THE EARLY YEARS of Ananda Village, Kirtani was part of the team of devotees who helped to establish the organic vegetable gardens there. Now a nayaswami and director of the Ananda Community near Assisi, Italy, Kirtani shared a beautiful story with us recently during our visit there.

One of the tasks for all the gardeners in those early days was to build huge compost piles to improve our infertile soil. These piles were assembled like giant cakes, by putting down consecutive layers of grass cut from the fields, organic kitchen waste, and a special mixture of bacteria that helped to break down the material into nutrient-rich compost.

One fall morning, it was Kirtani's task to "turn" the pile. This meant that she had to use a pitchfork to mix the upper layers with the lower ones, and the innermost parts of the pile with the outer ones. Mind you, these piles were about fifteen feet high, with a base of five by ten feet, so this was no easy job.

As she got to the inner part of the pile, where there was very little air circulation, she reached a layer of reeking kitchen waste. But worse than the odor, flies had laid their eggs inside the compost pile, and thousands of white maggots had hatched and lay squirming there. Repulsed by the sight and smell, Kirtani thought, "How can they stand to live in such a place?"

When the job was finally finished, Kirtani was glad to clean up, walk home for lunch, and forget the compost pile. It was a perfect fall day with a brilliant blue sky, luminous white clouds, and trees that seemed to be dancing in the sunlight. Rejoicing in the glorious sights around her, she thought, "How beautiful this all is!"

Suddenly Kirtani heard a voice within her say, "How can you stand to live in such a place?" Startled, she asked, "What do you mean? It's so beautiful!"

The divine voice responded, *"If you only knew what awaits you."*

Kirtani realized that from Divine Mother's perspective, this world was just as distasteful as the world of the maggots had seemed to her. She understood from the inner voice that a world of unimaginable beauty awaits us in God.

Paramhansa Yogananda gave poetic expression to that very thought:

Goodbye, blue house of heaven. Farewell, stars and celestial celebrities and your dramas on the screen of space. Goodbye, flowers with your traps of beauty and fragrance. You can hold me no longer. I am flying home.

The beauties of this world are but faint reflections of the true beauty that awaits us in our divine home, and all the sooner if we have the wisdom to seek it within now.

With joy and love,

Nayaswami Devi

THE GOLDEN RULE

September 8, 2016

A FEW DAYS AGO we participated in a very inspiring event. At our Ananda community near Assisi, Italy, we held a world peace conference in cooperation with a Japanese organization, World Peace Prayers Society, that promotes the Fuji Declaration, "calling for the rebirth of humanity's sacred spirit and a new civilization in which all life is connected as one." Devi and I were part of a panel of spiritual teachers that included a Buddhist monk, a Christian monk, the imam of Perugia, a leader from the Baha'i faith, as well as the founder of the International School of Forgiveness. As we sat together in our Temple of Light, we each spoke about how to promote peace and harmony among nations, religions, and individuals. The day ended movingly with a parade of flags and prayers for peace in every country on earth.

During my talk, I pointed out that respect for others is a theme addressed by all spiritual paths. Most scriptures have a version of the Golden Rule. Jesus Christ said it this way: "So in everything, do to others what you would have them do to you, for this sums up the Law and the Prophets."

But he was neither the first nor the last great soul to teach this truth. A friend recently gave me a card that made a deep impact on me. It had versions of the Golden Rule from many different faiths, echoing this simple truth, letting it reverberate again and again through time and space.

Our great master, Paramhansa Yogananda, repeated versions of the Golden Rule many times in his talks and writings. Here is a beautiful expression of the principle from his book, *Whispers from Eternity*:

Prayer for expanding Love from myself to all my brethren

O Divine Mother, teach me to use the gift of Thy love, which I feel in my heart, to love the members of my family more than myself. Bless me that I may love my neighbors more than my family. Expand my heart's feelings, that I love my country more than my neighbors, and *my world* and all my human brethren more than my country, neighbors, family, and my own self.

Lastly, teach me to love Thee more than anything else, for it is only Thy love that enables me to love everything. Without Thee, I could not love anything or anybody.

This teaching, though simple, has the potential to bring peace to the whole world. If we were simply to begin a personal practice of "doing to others what we would have others do to us," there would be no more war, nor violence, nor poverty. Through the practice of meditation we can actually experience our unity with others and truly feel that we are one world family.

As Mahatma Gandhi said, "We must become the change we want to see." If we want to help usher in a golden era for this fragile planet, let it begin with our very own daily practice of the Golden Rule.

In loving friendship,

Nayaswami Jyotish

THE FINAL STEP IN DISCIPLESHIP

September 15, 2016

PARAMHANSA YOGANANDA BEGAN his *Autobiography of a Yogi* with these words: "The characteristic features of Indian culture have long been a search for eternal verities and the concomitant disciple-guru relationship." For the Master to introduce his spiritual classic in this way shows the vital importance, in fact the inescapability, of discipleship in the search for God.

Sept. 12, 1948 was the day that Swami Kriyananda met his guru, Yoganandaji, for the first time. He knelt at the Master's feet, and with a heart filled with deep reverence and yearning said to him, "I want to be your disciple."

For the next sixty-five years until his passing in 2013, Swamiji lived the life of a devoted disciple: ever meditating on his guru's words and teachings, ever serving his guru's mission, and ever offering up all that he had or was at his guru's feet.

As we, in turn, came to Swamiji for his spiritual training as Master's disciples, we watched his discipleship deepen over the years, until it reached the point towards the end of his life when Swamiji said, "I no longer know where Kriyananda ends and Yogananda begins." As his attunement to Master grew, the vestiges of separation dissolved, and what remained was oneness in Spirit.

Discipleship involves many things: discipline, training and practice in the guru's teachings, service, self-offering—all of these and more. But ultimately, the guru-disciple relationship is rooted in divine love, a love unlike that found in any other human association. Master called it the "divine romance."

Those of us who knew Swamiji came to see that his relationship with Master was love brought to its highest expression. It was personal, but at the same time vast and all-embracing; precious, but meant to be shared with all. It changed the life of anyone who caught a glimpse of it, and enabled us to see our own potential capacity for limitless love. It was a yardstick of love and self-offering with which we could measure every aspect of our life.

Towards the end of his life Swamiji wrote an essay entitled, "Why I Love My Guru, Paramhansa Yogananda," which later was published in his book *Religion in the New Age*. There he wrote:

> His friendship for each of us was deeply personal, yet he was, for each of us, like a window onto infinity inviting us to "come outside" and merge in vastness.

> I love my Guru, as he himself wrote about his own guru Swami Sri Yukteswar, "as the spoken voice of silent God." He was ever, and is now more than ever, my nearest, dearest companion.

Thank you, beloved Swamiji, for showing us the way to God through perfected discipleship.

With gratitude,

Nayaswami Devi

A TOUCH OF LIGHT AND JOY

September 22, 2016

Toward the end of his life, Swami Kriyananda would often remark, "I feel so blissful, I can hardly contain it." We had seen him maintain a joyful spirit during many difficult times: temples collapsing or burning down, car accidents, health crises. No matter what was happening around him, Swamiji demonstrated that it didn't have the power to touch his inner Self.

Where does this ability to stay joyful no matter what life throws at us come from? It originates first from feeling your inner joy, and then developing the habit of bringing it back repeatedly during the day. Joy, you see, is our *natural state*—the most central of all the ways that God manifests Himself. So we don't need to create it, but merely to increase our awareness of it by removing the obscuring veils of self-involvement.

As with so many things in life, we can develop and maintain a buoyant consciousness if we apply ourselves. In order to bring joy under the control of our will, we must experience it both more deeply and more frequently. First we should try to *deepen* our experience of joy. This is best done in meditation, when the thoughts have been stilled. I would suggest that near the end of each meditation, you spend at least five minutes feeling a sense of joy and saturating your mind with a blissful vibration.

Secondly, we should try to feel touches of joy as often as possible throughout the day, until it becomes habitual. Don't wait for circumstances to make you happy: Learn to feel a happiness that needs no cause. One of Paramhansa Yogananda's most advanced disciples, Yogacharya Oliver Black, said he surrounded himself with a bubble of joy and never let anyone or anything pop his bubble.

This year members of Ananda are joining together in an experiment to see if we can deepen *our* consciousness of joy, and we invite you to join us. Each morning, spend at least five minutes toward the end of your meditation centering your awareness at the spiritual eye, seeing light there, and deeply feeling inner joy.

Then, as often as you remember, but at least five times during each day, reawaken the consciousness of light and joy with this technique: Stop, close your eyes, and bring your energy to the spiritual eye, at the point between the eyebrows. You may find it helpful to place your fingertip there to help you focus. Now become aware of light and joy at that point. Do this for at least fifteen seconds. This simple practice will reconnect you with the presence of God as light and joy. All success, all happiness, flows from a superconscious connection to the Divine. Master said that keeping our consciousness at the spiritual eye is the fastest way to make progress.

While quick and simple, this technique can have a profound effect on your well-being. Be a spiritual scientist, and see if a simple touch of light and joy can help you become blissful all the time.

In light and joy,

Nayaswami Jyotish

A DREAM OF THE FUTURE

September 29, 2016

I HAD AN INTRIGUING DREAM a few nights ago: It began as a conversation with a visionary scientist, reminiscent of Nikola Tesla, explaining to us his theories on the inner workings of the universe. Such conversations usually fly well over my head, but because he was communicating not with words but thought transference, I could easily understand his concepts.

I then said to him, "We must take you to see Ananda Village, where another kind of visionary thinking is being expressed." Immediately we were there, seemingly moving on thought waves, and found ourselves at the high school.

The teachers, students, buildings, and grounds were radiant with light and joy. Everyone was moving freely and harmoniously, as though in a beautifully choreographed dance, and even animals moved among them unafraid. But the strange thing was, I didn't recognize anyone or anything.

Although I felt Swami Kriyananda's presence, and knew I was at Ananda, I was puzzled and inwardly asked, "Where am I?" In an instant I knew: I was at the Ananda Village of the future, as Swamiji had envisioned it long ago, and knew that it would someday become.

I was thrilled at the thought that even with our own limited perspective and abilities, we had played a part in creating what was destined to be a beautiful way of life in the future.

In the late 1980s Swami Kriyananda wrote a book, *Cities of Light*. When I awoke from the dream, I began thinking of his words there:

Imagine a city—a beautiful city, such as a City of Tomorrow ought to be.

Imagine a community of people who know how to cooperate joyfully together, with kindness in their hearts for one another, and for all those whom their lives touch.

Imagine a city with schools that teach children the art of living, along with the standard offerings of academia; schools that teach them the meaning of success in human, and not in merely economic, terms; schools that teach them how to attract success, how to concentrate, how to overcome their negative moods, how to get along with others.

Imagine a City of Light. Here, the light sought is not material, merely, but is sought first in terms of expanded understanding and awareness.

"Such a place," perhaps you'll say, "may be imaginable. But is it *possible?*"

Such a community is now in existence and is called Ananda World Brotherhood Village. It is a prototype, an offering to others who may feel inspired to build on this example in their own way.

What has been accomplished so far is a reality. It remains a dream also, however, in the sense that, from these beginnings, others may create Cities of Light across the land—communities based on cooperation and friendship, high ideals, simple living, truth, and love for God.

I realized that my dream had allowed me to see the fulfillment of what Swamiji had seen all along. May we all help to make this dream of the future a reality.

Nayaswami Devi

THE GAME

October 6, 2016

THIS IS A STORY about the power of our thoughts. Some years ago I was playing a game of doubles in racquetball, meaning there are two players on each side. The object of the game is to keep the ball in play, trying to force the opposing team to make an error. Unfortunately, my partner was making most of the errors that evening. Although outwardly I tried to sound encouraging, inwardly I was thinking, "Can't he hit *anything* back?" As the game progressed, he got worse and worse, and my thoughts followed right along behind.

Then I remembered that our teachings tell us that our thoughts have the power to affect an outcome, and decided to test this out. I began to hold a positive mental image of him and inwardly compliment him with thoughts like, "He is really trying hard." When he did anything well, I mentally congratulated him.

Soon we began to win point after point. I don't remember whether or not we won that night, but I gained a huge inner victory. More important than outward results was the fact that, with a positive mindset, I began to *enjoy* the game. I learned from that experience that my negative thoughts not only hurt the outcome, but also hurt my partner, and made me unhappy as well.

This lesson is directly applicable in situations we face every day. If you want someone—a spouse, a child, a boss or coworker—to behave differently or perform better, then it is up to you to create a positive space for them to step into. If you can't, and remain inwardly critical, then you are part of the problem.

Here is a simple law: Positive thoughts produce positive results. Negative thoughts produce negative results.

There is a difference between discrimination and judgment. Discrimination sees something for what it is, while judgment includes an emotional component. It arises when something doesn't align with our *desires*. We might see that something is wrong, but if we go on to react judgmentally to it, then we have crossed over into quite another mindset. It usually means that we ourselves have that same issue, and are projecting expectations and self-criticism onto someone else.

In the *Autobiography of a Yogi*, Paramhansa Yogananda talks about an incident with his guru, Sri Yukteswar. Yogananda had left the ashram to go to the Himalayas and then returned some time later:

> "I am here, Guruji." My shamefacedness spoke more eloquently for me.
>
> "Let us go to the kitchen and find something to eat." Sri Yukteswar's manner was as natural as if hours and not days had separated us.
>
> "Master, I must have disappointed you by my abrupt departure from my duties here; I thought you might be angry with me."
>
> "No, of course not! Wrath springs only from thwarted desires. I do not expect anything from others, so their actions cannot be in opposition to wishes of mine. I would not use you for my own ends; I am happy only in your own true happiness."

In joy,

Nayaswami Jyotish

A gentle reminder to our regular readers: Remember to practice the Touch of Light and Joy at least five times each day.

MY PERSONAL JOURNEY WITH
AUTOBIOGRAPHY OF A YOGI

October 13, 2016

WE CAME INTO THE WORLD just weeks apart, *Autobiography of a Yogi* and I, born together in December 1946. Both of us were riding on waves of human hope: I was part of the "baby boomer" generation that emerged after millions of American servicemen returned from World War II. Hoping to leave the horrors of war behind, the soldiers wanted nothing more than to create a secure, prosperous life for their children.

And the *Autobiography* was published at the same time, when people were still reeling from the destruction that had been unleashed during the war. Many had lost faith, and in the war's aftermath were desperately hoping for answers: Is there any meaning in life? Is it possible for mankind to live in peace? Is there a God? Does He hear our prayers?

Paramhansa Yogananda's *Autobiography of a Yogi* and I both turn seventy this year. In the span of our shared lifetime many hopes have been fulfilled, but new challenges have arisen. Nevertheless, we have lived through this time together, and I'd like share with you our journey.

I first saw the *Autobiography*, with the picture of Yogananda on its cover, when I was about four years old. It was in a magazine advertisement for the book, and though I couldn't yet read, I remember staring at the photo of his face for a long time. "Is this a man or woman?" I wondered. His face and especially his eyes long remained impressed on my mind.

When I was eighteen, I read *A Passage to India* by E.M. Forster, which depicts the frustration and anguish of Indians and Westerners trying to understand and befriend each other. When I finished reading the book, I lay on my bed and cried for almost an hour. Though I didn't understand why at the time, I felt an overwhelming sadness that Easterners and Westerners couldn't find a way to come together.

Four years later, as a college student in Madison, Wisconsin, I was handed a copy of the *Autobiography*. As with most important events in my life, it took me a while to recognize the impact and significance that it would have for me over time. On my first attempt to read it, in May 1969, I bogged down: My mind was distracted and preoccupied with upcoming final exams, college graduation, and the question of what next to do with my life.

At the same time, a friend handed me a one-page flyer about Ananda Meditation Retreat in Northern California. It said that Ananda had been founded by a Swami Kriyananda, a direct disciple of Paramhansa Yogananda. "Aha," I thought as I read the flyer, "this could solve two of my problems." I could go to Ananda, take time to read the *Autobiography*, and sort out what I wanted to do next.

After finishing my last final I traveled to California, with a copy of the *Autobiography* as my only companion, to find the remote meditation retreat I'd read about in the flyer. Shortly after arriving on July 4,1969 (coincidentally the birthday of Ananda Village), I met Swami Kriyananda, who was to be my spiritual teacher, guide, and friend until his passing in 2013.

Coming to Ananda and meeting Kriyananda were, for me, the missing links that forged a living connection with the *Autobiography*. Through its pages I began to hear an inner voice that was deeply familiar and beloved—a voice that spoke of truths that I remembered and longed to know again.

This voice, rich with wisdom, subtlety, and humor, spoke of the need for uniting East and West, and for knowing God. It whispered in my soul, "If you want to feel my presence more deeply, get to know me in meditation." And this I did, beginning at that time a lifelong daily practice of meditation. Each time over the years when I've reread the *Autobiography*, this voice is at once familiar and somehow different, revealing ever more of its spiritual wisdom and beauty with each reading.

For years I have used this book as an oracle. Whenever I am faced with a problem in my life, I open the *Autobiography* three times at random. With amazing accuracy and in direct response to my question, the answer invariably appears in one of the three passages upon which my eyes fall.

Autobiography of a Yogi has been a living reality for me, always beckoning towards the summit where my soul longs to go. Nearly fifty years have passed since my first encounter, and I feel like I'm just beginning to know the book and its author.

And yet my journey doesn't end there. As my husband and I travel around the world sharing Yogananda's teachings, we meet literally thousands of people who have received inspiration and hope from this book.

I realize increasingly that we are all on the same journey with the *Autobiography*, and that the voice that first spoke in my heart so long ago speaks in the hearts of all who read it and want to listen. The book concludes with the sentence, "Lord, Thou hast given this monk a large family." Yogananda, in turn, has given that family to each of his devoted readers.

In Master's joy,

Nayaswami Devi

HOW *AUTOBIOGRAPHY OF A YOGI* CHANGED MY LIFE

October 20, 2016

*A*UTOBIOGRAPHY OF A YOGI changed my life. Really, it did. There is a power in that book that is far beyond the ordinary. Paramhansa Yogananda said to Swami Kriyananda on their first meeting, "I put my vibrations into it."

I read it when I was at one of the natural transition points in life, the changeover from school to adulthood. My studies had been a dry hole, never quite giving me the answers I was looking for. From my teens I was interested in the nature of consciousness, and as I grew older I studied psychology, hoping to find something that would show me the far horizon of human potential. I probably couldn't have articulated it at the time, but I was looking to unravel one of man's deepest questions: What is the purpose of life? I soon realized that what I was looking for lay far beyond the scope of school or psychology—that barren landscape (for me, at least) of lab rats, mental illness, and shallow sociological conclusions.

So, the day after my last college exam, I left Minneapolis for San Francisco, where I hoped to find a more supportive environment. My quest for expanded consciousness did not lie down the psychedelic streets of the hippie movement, but rather with the budding spiritual milieu. When in October 1966 I was "by chance" given a copy of *Autobiography of a Yogi*, it was a life-changing event for me. As I began reading, it seemed at first to be just one more in a long line of thought-provoking books. But as page after page resolved the very questions I had so long been asking, the book ascended from mere literature to scripture.

There were many things that I had a hard time accepting during that first reading, many things my doubting mind had to put on a shelf. But I had a deep underlying certainty that what Paramhansa Yogananda wrote was absolutely truthful. This was not someone teaching boring theories or secondhand concepts. What was written on those pages came from his personal experience and actual realization. Above all, it was Yogananda's transparent goodness and love that changed me. I wanted to experience what he wrote about, and he held out not only a vague hope, but the promise that someday I could. He showed how I could be a scientist conducting experiments in consciousness, and that my mind would be the laboratory. This I could relate to. This I could try. And so I have.

When I say that book changed my life, I mean it literally. Here are a few of the most important changes:

I moved from despair to hope, from someone with no clear direction in life to someone who now had a goal. Yogananda had showed me a pathway that I yearned to follow.

I changed from being an agnostic to someone who accepted that a Divine Intelligence was guiding everything.

I came to accept many things that my education, environment, and youthful cynicism had believed impossible. That book expanded not only the limits of human consciousness, but more importantly, *my* potential. Since that first reading I have found many saints and yogis who have had the same experiences. If they can, so can I. So can you.

Yogananda opened my heart, which until then had been dry and aching.

Most important of all, the book led me to Swami Kriyananda, my lifelong guide, mentor, friend, and supporter. He gave my life a spiritual and practical direction that started the day I met him, just a few months after *Autobiography of a Yogi* had shaken me awake. Swamiji's guiding hand continues to this day. I am grateful beyond the power of mere words to express.

I have long known that my experience is not unique, and that thousands of others have also had their lives changed by *Autobiography of a Yogi*. Is this also true for you, dear reader?

In deep gratitude,

Nayaswami Jyotish

THE BANANA TREE

October 27, 2016

As WE GATHERED IN the early-morning sunlight for group sadhana in Chennai, everyone was filled with eager anticipation of what lay ahead. After months of effort, we would officially be dedicating the new Center that evening, and friends would be gathering from all over India for the event.

As we went outside by the garden to do our Energization Exercises, the Southern Indian heat was already making itself felt. Just then a small tractor driven by two workmen noisily pulled up on the road outside the gate with a trailer hitched behind it. In it lay two long poles and two big stalks of the banana tree. Each stalk was about twenty feet tall, and was replete with a graceful stem, beautiful shiny leaves, a large bunch of still-green bananas, and a big purple flower at the end of the bunch.

The two workmen began to drive the poles into the ground on either side of the Center's entry gate, and then to lash the stalks to the poles.

Curious about what was happening, I asked one of my Chennai friends to explain. "The banana tree," Karthik told me, "is considered sacred. First, every part can be used: the fruit, peel, stem, and flower for food; the leaves for platters and, steamed, for wrapping food; the stem for juice and for fiber used in clothes and handicrafts; and the roots for medicinal purposes.

"Next, the banana is one of the few fruits that have no seeds, so it represents the soul freed of karma, with no compulsion to reincarnate. Finally, the banana tree is propagated by sending out shoots from the trunk, projecting its energy from itself to continue to serve others."

My friend went on to tell me that when a project is started— moving into a new house, for example, or starting a new business— banana stalks are often placed at the entrance to invite their sacred spirit to bless the building. In the next few days, now that my eyes knew what I was seeing, I began to spy banana stalks placed everywhere: in front of a huge new car dealership, straddling the entries to small shops along the road, and even little ones taped to the windshields of new cars.

I began to realize that we could learn a lot by emulating the beautiful, humble banana tree:

1. To give ourselves totally in service of others

2. To remove all seeds of karma and become free souls

3. To leave behind a legacy of our consciousness that reminds people to see the sacred everywhere

The Chennai Center dedication was a wonderful celebration, filled with many people, music, food, joy, and inspiration. But my eyes kept wandering over to the banana stalks, and inwardly I thanked them for their example, and for blessing Ananda's new home for God.

With joy,

Nayaswami Devi

HOW TO AVOID DOING YOUR DUTY

November 3, 2016

A MOTHER COMES INTO her son's bedroom and sees that he is still asleep.

"Wake up, wake up. It's late," she says.

The son responds by pulling the blankets up over his head.

"Wake up," his mother says again, "or you'll be late for school."

"I don't want to go to school," the son says, "and there are two reasons. All the children hate me, and all the teachers, they hate me, too."

"You still have to get up and go to school," his mother replies. "There are two reasons you have to go. You are fifty-one years old, and you are the principal."

I've told this joke in many different countries, and it always gets a big laugh. People relate to the whole scene; in fact, they've probably experienced something like it in their own lives—minus the punch line, of course. Everyone, at one time or another, has tried to avoid doing what they need to do.

Here are the two most common ways that you avoid doing your duty:

Sink into lethargy. You can go back to sleep or slump, couch potato–like, onto the sofa. Watching a lot of television or too many movies is also a good strategy. Then, of course, there is alcohol or drugs. Any of these things will block your energy enough to prevent you from acting. Afterwards, you can feel guilty, which is another good substitute for action. The only downside is that you will probably end up depressed.

Get distracted. This is another effective strategy to avoid doing what needs to be done. Find some important task, such as checking out the latest election news. It helps to carry several connected devices— a phone, a computer, a tablet—and use them all at the same time. Checking your devices every ten minutes or so will keep you from even remembering what you should be doing. Shopping is good, too. Really, any activity that takes a lot of time and has little benefit is a way to go.

Ramakrishna used the example of a school of fish caught in a net to show why so few of us transcend delusion. Some fish, the lethargic or tamasic kind, dive into the mud at the bottom, hoping to escape the net that way. Others, the second, rajasic type, swim madly about, crashing into the netting. Both of these types end up on someone's plate.

Only a very few fish swim toward the light, gathering enough speed to jump over the net to freedom. To do your duty—especially to escape delusion, your highest duty—takes focused, determined effort and the help of a guide.

A reporter once asked Swami Kriyananda if people really needed a guru. "No," he said surprising us all. "Why would you want someone telling you what to do?" He was, tongue in cheek, addressing the first two types. Then he continued, "Of course, if you want to find God, then you need a guru." The guru will give you the teachings, the tools, and the support, but you will have to do the work.

So, my friends, I have given you two good strategies for dodging your duty and one for fulfilling it. The net is around us. What will you do?

In joyful friendship,

Nayaswami Jyotish

BUILDING SPIRITUAL POWER AGAINST TROUBLED TIMES*

November 10, 2016

AMERICA HAS MADE ITS CHOICE now in this presidential election. The world may well be facing troubled times, as the United States and all nations come to terms with a dramatic break from past values and models of government. Already waves of uncertainty, confusion, and fear are moving across the planet.

But whether the outcome was your personal choice or not, the question arises: "What do we do now?"

As global citizens we need to move into the future as positively as possible to help establish stability in these changing times. America was the first nation to be founded on higher principles of equality and human rights, and we need to uphold these ideals.

As devotees, we have a further responsibility. We must give our full strength to keeping our consciousness uplifted, holding God's presence in our hearts and minds, and helping others to do the same.

Make the Right Choices Now

Learn to love heroically. Some years ago Swami Kriyananda shared with us a dream he'd had about impending world disasters. The message he received was that our answer to what lies ahead should be to "love heroically." Try to act as expansively and selflessly as you can, and resist the pull to think of your own needs first. In hundreds of little ways throughout each day choose selflessness and kindness over self-interest and narrow-mindedness.

Even more than that, resist the temptation to contract your heart. Find a deeper capacity to love all unconditionally, with acceptance

---

* This is the title of a talk by Swami Kriyananda (available for free download at treasuresalongthepath.com/building-spiritual-power).

and without judgment. This is what the lives of all great spiritual teachers demonstrate for us.

Give more dynamic focus to your meditation. Practice the techniques of our line of gurus with increased dedication and fervor. Add a longer meditation to your sadhana each week. The attunement with higher consciousness that comes through deep meditation is our greatest aid, giving us the strength, wisdom, and calmness to deal with whatever may come.

Through this deepened attunement we also become clearer channels for higher consciousness in all of our activities. Be especially aware of expressing God and Guru in all your words and actions.

Deepen your connection with other devotees. Seek out and associate with like-minded people who are also striving to live in the light. Avoid negative discussions or arguments about whose opinions are right or wrong. This will only keep you enmeshed in maya.

If you are near an Ananda Meditation Center or Community, start attending more regularly. If you are already active in one, begin attending more group meditations and prayer sessions. Do Yoganandaji's prayer for world peace and harmony with others regularly.

If there is no Ananda center close by, then join our Virtual Community online. This will lend tremendous support to your efforts to keep your consciousness rooted in peace. When we gather together with other devotees in these ways, we not only uplift our own lives, but also draw blessings to the world.

Cling to what is real and eternal. The affairs of this world, even of a great nation like America, are in the final analysis fleeting shadows on the screen of time. The only real, lasting things are God's Peace, Joy, and Love. When moments of uncertainty, fear, or discouragement pull at you, remember to look past the shadows to the Divine Light constantly illuminating everything.

God is calling us now to build our own spiritual power. Let's grasp this opportunity with energy and enthusiasm, and understand that it's the dharma we chose for this incarnation.

In Master's love,

Nayaswami Devi

A MIRACLE OF PROTECTION

November 17, 2016

SOMETIMES WE HAVE DOUBTS. Does God really care about us? Does He love us or protect us when we are unable to fend for ourselves? I heard an amazing account that shows that God and Guru are there when we most need them. Here is the story, as told to our center leader from Pune, India, and relayed to Devi and me this morning. It happened in 2014 to a young man in Ahmedabad, in the Indian state of Gujarat.

The young man was very good at business and became rich while still quite young. But his quick rise created jealousy among some of his rivals, and one day they falsely accused him of cheating. The papers picked up and printed the juicy story. The next morning when his parents read the account (he was still living at home), they threw him out of the house. At the bank, he found that his account and all of his credit cards had been frozen. From one day to the next, he found himself abandoned and nearly penniless.

Stunned, wandering, and hungry, he stopped at a roadside stall to buy some food with his few rupees. As he was standing there a young monk in orange robes came up to him and said, "The food here is not very healthy." The young man replied that it was all he could afford.

The monk said, "Come with me, and I will feed you," and proceeded to take him to a nearby Kali temple where he was given a sumptuous meal.

By this time it was evening, and his new friend asked, "Where are you staying?"

The young man replied sadly, "I have nowhere to stay."

The orange-robed monk said, "Come with me. You can stay at my ashram."

They proceeded to a nearby ashram of Yogoda Sat-Sangha, where the monk led him to a room and fed him once again. In the morning, as the young man was leaving, a guard stopped him and asked what he was doing there. The young man explained that a monk had given him a room for the night. The guard said, "Visitors are not permitted to stay here. And besides, no monks are here at this time."

The young man, quite bewildered, pointed to the cover photo of a nearby *Autobiography of a Yogi,* and said, "There, that is the monk who helped me." He was, of course, astounded to learn that the man who had helped him had been "dead" for over sixty years.

Soon his denouncers were themselves denounced. The man quickly regained his wealth, and went on to achieve even greater success.

But a question arises: What drew Master to protect this man, who had never even heard his name? One reason might be that ever since he was a mere child, this man had had an implicit faith in the Divine. Or perhaps it was his karma due to a past-life connection with Yogananda.

But there is another possible explanation that I find more interesting and compelling. Maybe this story of God and Guru's grace is meant for you and for me. Are *we* not in need of reassurance and help from time to time? Perhaps this miracle was performed not only to help that young man, but also so that his story could reach you at this very moment and show, once again, that Master is watching, loving, and protecting each of us in the hour of our need.

In gratitude to the Divine,

Nayaswami Jyotish

ARE YOU A SPIRITUAL SUCCESS?

November 24, 2016

Recently while in Pune, India, I asked an old friend how he felt he'd changed spiritually over the years. He replied, "It's hard to see change from one day to the next, but looking back I see that I'm not the same person I used to be, though my nature remains much the same. In the past I used to be skeptical about everything, but now doubt has nearly disappeared as God and Guru's presence has grown. I may still question things in order to understand them better, but I'm no longer plagued with a doubting nature."

How can we evaluate our own spiritual success? Paramhansa Yogananda says, "Success is measured by your level of happiness, by your ability to remain in peaceful harmony with divine laws." Here are some of Yoganandaji's principles for success:

Take advantage of the spiritual opportunities given to you. To be drawn to a true guru and receive techniques for liberation is a result of very good past karma. Accept that you've earned these blessings by efforts in other lifetimes. Now continue to deepen and refine your understanding of the teachings and techniques of the path of Kriya Yoga.

Feel that meditation is not something foreign to you, but is a familiar practice that you're now picking up once again. Resolve that in this lifetime you will finish the job and find inner freedom.

Habitual positive or negative thoughts determine our spiritual success or failure. Never allow yourself to dwell on past unsuccessful efforts, but daily water your meditation with fresh enthusiasm and hope.

Yoganandaji said, "The season of failure is the best time for sowing the seeds of success." Whatever has happened in the past, know that it has brought you one step closer to the realization of God's presence. Releasing the power of positive thought and giving our spiritual efforts "one more try" is a tremendous help in achieving success.

Spiritual success requires dynamic, rather than mechanical, will power. Mechanical will power is found in any unthinking, habitual action that requires little initiative or energy on our part. By contrast, dynamic will power involves conscious determination and effort.

To develop it, challenge yourself to do things that you thought you couldn't accomplish. Start with small achievements, and then gradually, concentrating on one thing at a time, build your dynamic will power by taking on bigger tasks. Eventually you'll be able to direct this flow of determined energy to accomplish whatever you set out to do—especially to finding God.

Attunement with Divine Consciousness is the most important factor in success. By attuning our consciousness with God and Guru, we open ourselves to the flow of their magnetism. The guru's magnetism realigns the "molecules" of our past karmic tendencies upward towards God, rather than allowing the "thwarting cross-currents of ego" to pull our consciousness downward.

Yoganandaji wrote: "When you continue to seek God no matter what obstacles arise, you are using human will in its highest form. You will thus operate the law of success known to the ancient sages who found God."

Of all human endeavors, the only one in which everyone can reach the top is the search for God. Let us all continue our efforts, until we can say, "God and Guru have blessed me with true spiritual success."

In divine friendship,

Nayaswami Devi

TWO GREAT MASTERS

December 1, 2016

TODAY WAS A REMARKABLE DAY! We are in Puri, India, where Swami Sri Yukteswar had an ashram, and where his body is enshrined in a small *samadhi mandir* (shrine that holds the body of a great master). Paramhansa Yogananda used often to come here with his guru, and it was in Puri that Sri Yukteswar left his body in 1936.

This morning we had a wonderful meditation in this shrine. There is a remarkable presence in any place where a great saint has spent time, and an even more powerful effect if his body is still there. All religions recognize the spiritual power that lingers in such places, and often the vast temples or cathedrals that are built to honor them become important pilgrimage spots. But Sri Yukteswar's shrine is small and modest, befitting the inward nature of the yogic path.

As a small group of us meditated there, I felt an aura of deep peace. It was easier to concentrate and to do Kriya and other techniques that had been practiced and taught by the great master. It was as if Sri Yukteswar was silently helping us to turn our minds inward.

In the stories in *Autobiography of a Yogi* Sri Yukteswar always seemed a stern disciplinarian, and I must confess that of all the masters of our path, he has been the hardest for me to approach. But last year I was leading a meditation at one of our centers in India, and as I prayed to him I felt a little twinge of sadness that I couldn't seem to bridge that gap. Just then, the garland that was around his picture inexplicably fell off. As I lovingly placed it around his image once again, I knew that he had reached out to me, and I gave a silent prayer in thanks for this tiny miracle. Since then I have felt much closer to him.

After our time with Sri Yukteswar, we went to the samadhi mandir of Totapuri, the guru of the great master Ramakrishna. At one time Ramakrishna was struggling to attain the highest state of consciousness and to go beyond God in form. He regularly had visions of

Divine Mother in the form of the goddess Kali, and would go into ecstasy, but in his worship of her he could not go into the formless state.

Totapuri instructed him to mentally take a sword and slice through the form of Kali when she appeared to him. That evening, as Ramakrishna began to worship her, Totapuri took a small piece of glass and ground it into the point between Ramakrishna's eyebrows, saying, "Concentrate here! Take a mental sword and cut through her!" He did as Totapuri instructed, and went into the highest samadhi beyond all forms of maya.

We were also able to meditate for a long time at Totapuri's ashram, and to meditate as well in his little bedroom. Again we felt a remarkable power enfolding us. As we were leaving, the resident monk took us to a banyan tree. Totapuri had instructed two disciples to meditate inside the hanging roots of this tree for three days, and both of them went into samadhi. The tree itself felt sacred, as if it too had participated in that event.

Such are the stories one hears in this remarkable country of India and in this holy city, the home from ancient times of the famous Jagannath Temple.

In joy,

Nayaswami Jyotish

CROSSING A THRESHOLD OPENED LONG AGO

December 8, 2016

WE WERE SITTING on the beach our first evening in Puri, India, gazing at the moonlight on the waves and listening to the crashing of the surf on the shore. Seventy devotees would be joining us in two days for a pilgrimage to sacred sites in this area, which is considered to be one of the holiest in India.

A friend who was sitting with us asked, "When was the last time you were in Puri?" Thinking about it, I realized that I hadn't fully grasped the significance of the timing of our visit. Quietly I replied, "Twenty years ago in 1996 with Swami Kriyananda."

In the fall of 1996, Swamiji had invited a small group of us to accompany him to India. One of the places we visited was Puri, especially sacred to Paramhansa Yogananda's followers, because it was here that his guru, Swami Sri Yukteswar, left his body in 1936. It was here also that Master placed the lifeless form of his guru in a small *samadhi mandir* on the grounds of the Karar ashram. And there his body still resides.

As we were meditating with Swami Kriyananda at that mandir in 1996, I glanced over and saw him absorbed in a state of profound interiorization and concentration. It seemed that with all his being he was asking Sri Yuktewar's blessings on his search for God. Later, when we were all getting ready to leave, we knelt before Swamiji and asked him to bless our discipleship, which he did, lovingly and unassumingly.

Now twenty years later we returned to the mandir, and in the "easy resurrection of memory" I could see Swamiji sitting there in deep self-offering. As we began to meditate, Sri Yukteswar's spiritual vitality and power washed over us like a great wave, and I felt as though we were crossing an inner threshold that Swamiji had opened for us long ago through his blessing. Our spiritual development unfolds over time in ways of which we are rarely aware, but in this case we caught a glimpse of the cause-and-effect process that draws us forward.

We will be leaving India in a few days to return to America. We've seen much spiritual beauty and depth here that cannot help but leave a permanent impression on the mind. But among all the inner treasures that India has bestowed, I will especially cherish our time in Puri when we glimpsed this simple truth:

When God created each of us, He also set into play a unique plan for how we would return to Him. This plan is already underway for every one of us, and will be fulfilled when the time is right. All that is needed in the meantime is our trust in Him.

Your friend in God,

Nayaswami Devi

CHRISTMAS IMAGES AND THEIR
SPIRITUAL MEANING

December 15, 2016

MANY POPULAR IMAGES associated with Christmas are actually rooted in inner spiritual realities. But over time the deeper meaning becomes lost, and the symbol becomes an end unto itself. Perhaps the most iconic symbols are the Christmas tree and Santa Claus.

The use of evergreen wreaths goes back to the prehistory of Egypt, Greece, and Rome, while the more modern decorated Christmas tree was established in medieval Europe. The origins of Santa Claus go back to Saint Nicholas, a fourth-century Christian bishop in Greece famous for giving gifts to the poor.

The modern image of Santa was popularized by the famous poem beginning "'Twas the night before Christmas . . . ," published in 1823. Our visual image comes from the illustrator Thomas Nast and his drawing of Santa Claus done in 1881, which was later adapted by others for use in advertising. From these roots has grown the jolly man with a red suit, a big belly, and a long, white beard who lives at the North Pole and brings gifts to children who have been good.

But as yogis, it is helpful to look past these cultural symbols and see the inner essence they represent. In this deeper sense, Santa Claus represents deeply seated spiritual memories—a sort of collective consciousness of our divine nature. God dwells within us, especially in the upper (north) chakras, and is joyful, benevolent, and the giver of the gifts of all good qualities and life itself.

The Christmas tree is an outer symbol of the astral spine and the chakras. The tree is an evergreen, maintaining its leaves throughout the winter, and therefore represents immortality. The lights, bulbs, and other ornaments represent inner lights and qualities. Gifts are spiritualized by appropriately being placed underneath the tree, much as they might be placed at the foot of an altar in another culture.

But the outer symbols lose their deeper meaning unless we balance them with inner realization. At Ananda we achieve this balance by celebrating "spiritual Christmas" with an all-day meditation where we try to merge with the Christ Consciousness. This is followed by "social Christmas," with the usual parties and gift giving. By honoring both inner and outer realities, we find a lovely sense of integration in our lives.

Paramhansa Yogananda expressed this beautifully: "Exchange gifts with the thought of Christ and the thought of giving Him the gift of your heart and receiving the gift of Himself on the Christmas Tree of your calm consciousness, richly decorated and glistening with the Soul-qualities of all those you have met and loved. Through the portal of your meditation, let your imprisoned joy escape to, and rest in, the heart of Christ, which is in everything. Let your joy dance in the farthest planets, over the vastness of the blue, and in the nearest waves of your love. Then you will behold Christ cradled in every manifest thing."

Happy Christmas

Nayaswami Jyotish

THE SECOND COMING OF CHRIST

December 22, 2016

IN THIS CHRISTMAS SEASON, it's important to reflect on the deeper message of Christ's life and birth. Paramhansa Yogananda told his disciples that it was Jesus himself who appeared to Babaji in the Himalayas, and asked him to send these teachings to the West in order to reveal the deeper meaning of Christianity. Through people's practice of meditation, they could experience Jesus as a living reality—a being with whom they can commune, rather than merely read about in the Bible.

Yoganandaji went on to explain that, contrary to common Christian beliefs, this is what Jesus meant when he said that he would come again. "The Second Coming of Christ" is how Yogananda often referred to his mission, for it teaches people how to fulfill the true promise of Jesus—not to return again in physical form, but in the souls of those who love him and commune with him.

Following the path brought by our great line of masters—Jesus Christ, Babaji, Lahiri Mahasaya, Sri Yukteswar, and Yoganandaji—is a blessing beyond faculty of words to express. It holds the promise of divine love and protection, of inner guidance and assurance, and ultimately of final soul freedom. But it also holds a responsibility for each one of us, for to be a true disciple we must try to fulfill the purpose for which these masters came.

This means working towards the kind of inner transformation in which we no longer live in our limited ego, but rather in our expanded soul nature; in which we no longer focus on the darkness of this world, but rather see the light of God shining everywhere. And ultimately this means awakening within ourselves the universal Christ Consciousness, which is the true "Second Coming of Christ."

When we take up the banner of our Guru's mission as our own personal calling, then we feel his true stamp of approval on our discipleship.

In his book *Revelations of Christ*, Swami Kriyananda writes: "I myself believe in Paramhansa Yogananda's prediction of 'a new world of peace, harmony, and prosperity for all,' when people give up fighting the inevitable and learn to accept, and even to love, one another, and then to work together for the common weal.

"Then will the Second Coming of Christ become a reality: not necessarily the return of Jesus the man, but of the principles for which he stood bravely and, eventually, died on the cross."

We wish you all a happy and blessed Christmas season, and send our sincere prayer that "the light of Christ shine upon you."

In God, Christ, and Guru,

Nayaswami Devi

HOW TO BE A DIVINE SCULPTOR

December 29, 2016

I N A FEW DAYS it will be a new year, 2017, and it's time to think about changes you might like to make. An artist once was asked how he could sculpt such a perfect image of an elephant. He replied, "It's easy. I just chip away everything that doesn't look like an elephant." We need to chip away everything that doesn't look like the saint we want to become.

There is much spiritually to be learned from one of the most famous of all sculptures, Michelangelo's *David*. Here are a few techniques and attitudes that will help you resolve in this new year to conquer the Goliath on the spiritual path:

Give 100%: Michelangelo used every bit of the giant piece of Carrara marble that he was given by the Commune of Florence. In fact, there is a slight flat area in the back where there was not enough marble to finish the curve of a shoulder. *Our spiritual takeaway: At birth, you were given certain talents, tendencies, and limitations from past lives. Use all of yourself in your spiritual quest.*

Stay true to your own vision: There is a famous story: When Michelangelo had completed his masterpiece, the city officials who had commissioned the giant David came to visit and view it. An officer criticized the shape of the nose. The wily sculptor climbed up the scaffold, secretly holding a handful of marble dust. While pretending to chisel the nose, he let the dust fall from his hand. The official looked again and said, "Yes, now it is perfect." *Our spiritual takeaway: Others—parents, friends, co-workers—may want to mold you according to their vision, not your own. On the spiritual quest, you must always be true to yourself.*

Use your strengths, ignore your weaknesses: Michelangelo purposely exaggerated the size of David's hands and head, to better portray his capabilities for the upcoming battle. *Our spiritual takeaway: Don't be afraid of seeming a bit unbalanced. You will need all your talents to* *achieve your spiritual goal. Ignore most of your weaknesses—you could spend all your time trying to improve them only to achieve mediocrity.*

Prepare yourself for battle: David is portrayed just before his battle, using a motif called "immanent action" that artists from ancient times have used to heighten tension. David's physical posture is relaxed, but his head, eyes, and demeanor show intense concentration and determination. *Our spiritual takeaway: We must prepare ourselves mentally and through proper attitudes if we hope to conquer maya, the apparently impossible enemy in front of us.*

Don't fight maya on its own terms: In his book *David and Goliath*, Malcolm Gladwell points out that David's victory was assured as soon as he chose to fight. In ancient warfare, a warrior such as Goliath fought against other foot-soldiers with a sword and shield. Someone with a sling, such as David, stood back at a distance and hurled his stone, more like an artillery man. As soon as David stepped onto the field, the onlookers realized that he would win. It was the change of tactics that was key. *Our spiritual takeaway: In our sadhana we must change our tactics—we can't think our way or will our way out of delusion. Our techniques are not meant to help us win the battle in maya's realm, to make us rich or powerful, for instance. Our practices instead help to withdraw our life-force and go beyond delusion altogether. And yet, we need to continue to fight the battle because, unlike a static marble sculpture that stays unchanged for centuries, we continually either progress or regress.*

Choose the right model: A dear friend, Devi Mukherjee, wrote a book called *Shaped by Saints.* In his youth he'd decided that he wanted his life to be molded by true gurus, and he spent a great deal of time in the company of the great ones. A great master, such as Paramhansa Yogananda, comes in order to serve as a model of how to live an ideal life, in tune with God's will. As he said, "O Divine Sculptor, chisel Thou my life according to Thy design!"

In joy,

Nayaswami Jyotish

ABOUT THE AUTHORS

Jyotish and Devi Novak are spiritual teachers, writers, and counselors. They travel and lecture extensively throughout the world on the topics of yoga, meditation, family, and living the spiritual life. They are disciples of Paramhansa Yogananda, (author of *Autobiography of a Yogi*), and have served together as spiritual directors of Ananda Worldwide since 1984. They are also members of the Nayaswami Order founded by Swami Kriyananda, the founder also of Ananda Worldwide. They are co-authors of *Touch of Light*.

Nayaswami Jyotish was named by Swami Kriyananda as his spiritual successor after decades of helping him build Ananda's work around the world. Jyotish began taking classes from Swami Kriyananda in 1967, and together in 1969 they moved to the rural property in the foothills of the Sierra Nevada mountains of California that is now a model spiritual community: Ananda Village.

Swami Jyotish has lectured throughout the world and has helped establish Ananda's work in Italy and India. He has also written several books: *Lessons in Meditation, How to Meditate, 30-Day Essentials for Marriage,* and *30-Day Essentials for Career.*

Nayaswami Devi first met Swami Kriyananda in 1969 and dedicated her life to the spiritual path. She and Jyotish were married in 1975, and have spent their life together serving Kriyananda and their guru, Paramhansa Yogananda, through teaching and outreach around the world. Devi is the author of *Faith Is My Armor: The Life of Swami Kriyananda* and editor of two of Kriyananda's books: *Intuition for Starters* and *The Light of Superconsciousness.*

Dear Reader,

Ananda is a worldwide work based on the same teachings expressed in this book—those of the great spiritual teacher Paramhansa Yogananda. If you enjoyed this title, Crystal Clarity Publishers invites you to continue to deepen your spiritual life through the many avenues of Ananda Worldwide—including meditation communities, centers, and groups; online virtual community and webinars; retreat centers offering classes and teacher training in yoga and meditation; and more.

For special offers and discounts for first-time visitors to Ananda, visit: http://www.crystalclarity.com/welcome

Feel free to contact us. We are here to serve you.

Joy to you,

Crystal Clarity Publishers

ANANDA WORLDWIDE

Ananda, a worldwide organization founded by Swami Kriyananda, offers spiritual support and resources based on the teachings of Paramhansa Yogananda. There are Ananda spiritual communities in Nevada City, Sacramento, and Palo Alto, California; Seattle, Washington; Portland and Laurelwood, Oregon; as well as a retreat center and European community in Assisi, Italy, and a community near New Delhi, India. Ananda supports more than 140 meditation groups worldwide.

For more information about Ananda's work, our communities, or meditation groups near you, please call 530.478.7560 or visit www. ananda.org.

THE EXPANDING LIGHT

The Expanding Light is the largest retreat center in the world to share exclusively the teachings of Paramhansa Yogananda. Situated in the Ananda Village community, it offers the opportunity to experience spiritual life in a contemporary ashram setting. The varied, year-round schedule of classes and programs on yoga, meditation, and spiritual practice includes Karma Yoga, Personal Retreat, Spiritual Travel, and online learning. The Ananda School of Yoga & Meditation offers certified yoga, yoga therapist, spiritual counselor, and meditation teacher trainings. Large groups are welcome.

The teaching staff are experts in Kriya Yoga meditation and all aspects of Yogananda's teachings. All staff members live at Ananda Village and bring an uplifting approach to their areas of service. The serene natural setting and delicious vegetarian meals help provide an ideal environment for a truly meaningful visit.

For more information, please call 800.346.5350
or visit www.expandinglight.org.

CRYSTAL CLARITY PUBLISHERS

Crystal Clarity Publishers offers many additional resources to assist you in your spiritual journey, including many other books (see the following pages for some of them), a wide variety of inspirational and relaxation music composed by Swami Kriyananda, and yoga and meditation videos. To request a catalog, place an order for the above products, or to find more information, please contact us at:

Crystal Clarity Publishers / www.crystalclarity.com
14618 Tyler Foote Rd. / Nevada City, CA 95959
TOLL FREE: 800.424.1055 or 530.478.7600 FAX: 530.478.7610
EMAIL: clarity@crystalclarity.com

Visit our website for our online catalog, with secure ordering.

HOW TO BE HAPPY ALL THE TIME

The Wisdom of Yogananda Series, VOLUME 1
Paramhansa Yogananda

Yogananda powerfully explains virtually everything needed
to lead a happier, more fulfilling life. Topics include: looking
for happiness in the right places; choosing to be happy; tools
and techniques for achieving happiness; sharing happiness with others; balancing success and happiness; and many more.

TOUCH OF LIGHT

Living the teachings of Paramhansa Yogananda
Jyotish and Devi Novak

The great spiritual master, Paramhansa Yogananda (author of
Autobiography of a Yogi), offered teachings that can transform
our spiritual lives. *Touch of Light* reveals some of the many
ways Yogananda's teachings can benefit us. Each chapter contains a jewel of
wisdom that can speed you forward on your spiritual path. Jyotish and Devi
Novak are close students of Yogananda's disciple, Swami Kriyananda, and
Spiritual Directors of Ananda Sangha Worldwide.

HOW TO MEDITATE

A Step-by-Step Guide to the Art & Science of Meditation
Jyotish Novak

This clear and concise guidebook contains everything you
need to start your practice. With easy-to-follow instructions,
meditation teacher Jyotish Novak demystifies meditation—presenting the
essential techniques so that you can quickly grasp them. Since it was first
published in 1989, *How to Meditate* has helped thousands to establish a
regular meditation routine. This newly revised edition includes a bonus
chapter on scientific studies showing the benefits of meditation, plus all-
new photographs and illustrations.

CHANGE YOUR MAGNETISM, CHANGE YOUR LIFE

How to Eliminate Self-Defeating Patterns and Attract True Success
Naidhruva Rush

Success in every area depends on the strength and quality of
your magnetism. Discover how to release the enormous energy
latent within and direct it one-pointedly toward whatever you
want to achieve.

The original 1946 unedited edition of Yogananda's spiritual masterpiece

AUTOBIOGRAPHY OF A YOGI
Paramhansa Yogananda

Autobiography of a Yogi is one of the best-selling Eastern philosophy titles of all time, with millions of copies sold, named one of the best and most influential books of the twentieth century. This highly prized reprinting of the original 1946 edition is the only one available free from textual changes made after Yogananda's death. Yogananda was the first yoga master of India whose mission was to live and teach in the West.

In this updated edition are bonus materials, including a last chapter that Yogananda wrote in 1951, without posthumous changes. This new edition also includes the eulogy that Yogananda wrote for Gandhi, and a new foreword and afterword by Swami Kriyananda, one of Yogananda's close, direct disciples.

Also available in unabridged audiobook (MP3) format, read by Swami Kriyananda.

30-DAY ESSENTIALS FOR MARRIAGE
Jyotish Novak

The inspirational ideas in this full-color gift book are fun, simple ways to enhance your marriage, helping you improve your life together in just thirty days—one thought for each day of the month.

Featuring one inspiring piece of advice and one practical exercise per day, this book is a useful, lighthearted, and eye-catching way for couples—whether engaged, newly married, or together for years—to quickly and gently deepen their relationship.

30-DAY ESSENTIALS FOR CAREER
Jyotish Novak

Find, build, and sustain a successful career. These inspirational ideas are simple, effective ways to improve your working life. Discover the essentials of a satisfying career in just thirty days—one thought for each day of the month.

Featuring one inspiring piece of advice and one practical exercise per day, this book is a useful and enjoyable guide for improving your working life now.

231

Paramhansa Yogananda
A Biography with Personal Reflections
and Reminiscences
Swami Kriyananda

The New Path
My Life with Paramhansa Yogananda
Swami Kriyananda

Demystifying Patanjali
*The Wisdom of Paramhansa Yogananda Presented
by his direct disciple, Swami Kriyananda*

The Essence of Self-Realization
*The Wisdom of Paramhansa Yogananda
Recorded, Compiled, and Edited by
his disciple, Swami Kriyananda*

Conversations with Yogananda
*Recorded, with Reflections, by his
disciple, Swami Kriyananda*

Revelations of Christ
*Proclaimed by Paramhansa Yogananda
Presented by his disciple, Swami Kriyananda*

The Essence of the Bhagavad Gita
*Explained by Paramhansa Yogananda
As Remembered by his disciple, Swami Kriyananda*

Whispers from Eternity
*Paramhansa Yogananda
Edited by his disciple, Swami Kriyananda*

The Rubaiyat of Omar Khayyam
*Paramhansa Yogananda
Edited by his disciple, Swami Kriyananda*

–The Wisdom of Yogananda series–
How to Be Happy All the Time
Karma and Reincarnation
How to Love and Be Loved
How to Be a Success
How to Have Courage, Calmness, and
Confidence
How to Achieve Glowing Health and Vitality
How to Achieve Your True Potential
The Man Who Refused Heaven

Meditation for Starters with CD
Swami Kriyananda

Intuition for Starters
Swami Kriyananda

Through the Chakras
Savitri Simpson

Through Many Lives
Savitri Simpson

Chakras for Starters
Savitri Simpson

Vegetarian Cooking for Starters
Diksha McCord

The Art and Science of Raja Yoga
Swami Kriyananda

Awaken to Superconsciousness
Swami Kriyananda

Living Wisely, Living Well
Swami Kriyananda

The Bhagavad Gita
*According to Paramhansa Yogananda
Edited by his disciple, Swami Kriyananda*

Stories of Yogananda's Youth
Swami Kriyananda

Secrets of Success and Leadership
Swami Kriyananda

Self-Expansion Through Marriage
Swami Kriyananda

The Time Tunnel
Swami Kriyananda

The Yugas
Joseph Selbie & David Steinmetz

God Is for Everyone
*Inspired by Paramhansa Yogananda
As taught to and understood by his
disciple, Swami Kriyananda*

Religion in the New Age
Swami Kriyananda

Money Magnetism
J. Donald Walters (Swami Kriyananda)

In Divine Friendship
Swami Kriyananda

Deep Nature Play
Joseph Cornell

Sharing Nature
Joseph Cornell

The Sky and Earth Touched Me
Joseph Cornell

Listening to Nature
Joseph Cornell

Education for Life
J. Donald Walters (Swami Kriyananda)

The Meaning of Dreaming
Savitri Simpson

The Healing Kitchen
Diksha McCord

Love Perfected, Life Divine
Swami Kriyananda

Walking With William of Normandy
A Paramhansa Yogananda Pilgrimage Guide
Richard Salva

Swami Kriyananda: A Life in God
Swami Kriyananda

Secrets of Meditation and Inner Peace
Swami Kriyananda

The Need for Spiritual Communities
and How to Start Them
Swami Kriyananda

The Yoga of Abraham Lincoln
Richard Salva

A Healer's Handbook
Mary Kretzmann

Divine Will Healing
Mary Kretzmann

The Four Stages of Yoga
Nischala Cryer

Solving Stress
Satyaki Kraig Brockschmidt

The Yoga of Ghost Hunting
Richard Salva

Blessed Lanfranc
Richard Salva

Stories of Swamiji
Richard Salva

Soul Journey from Lincoln
to Lindbergh
Richard Salva

From Bagels to Curry
Lila Devi

The Joyful Athlete
George Beinhorn

Finding Happiness
Swami Kriyananda

The Flawless Mirror
Kamala Silva

Ananda Yoga for Higher Awareness
Swami Kriyananda

The Light of Superconsciousness
Swami Kriyananda

Ask Asha
Asha Praver

Loved and Protected
Asha Praver

The Light of Christ Within
Elena Joan Cara and John Laurence

Spiritual Yoga
Gyandev McCord

A Tale of Songs
Swami Kriyananda

A Pilgrimage to Guadalupe
Swami Kriyananda

AUM: The Melody of Love
Joseph Bharat Cornell

A Fight for Religious Freedom
Jon R. Parsons

Yogananda for the World
Swami Kriyananda

Affirmations for Self-Healing
Swami Kriyananda

The Art of Supportive Leadership
J. Donald Walters (Swami Kriyananda)

The Pilgrim's France
A Pilgrim's Guide to the Saints
James and Colleen Heater

Two Souls: Four Lives
Catherine Kairavi

The Beatitudes
Swami Kriyananda

Your Sun Sign as a Spiritual Guide
Swami Kriyananda